For the Love of My Son

For the Love of My Son

*A mother's harrowing journey
in search of justice*

Margaret Davis

with Jane Ross-Macdonald

HODDER

Names have been changed
to protect identities, throughout

Copyright © 2006 by Margaret Davis

First published in Great Britain in 2006 by Hodder & Stoughton
A division of Hodder Headline

The right of Margaret Davis to be identified as the Author
of the Work has been asserted by her in accordance with
the Copyright, Designs and Patents Act 1988.

A Hodder paperback

1

A CIP catalogue record for this title is available from the British Library

ISBN 978 0 340 899007
ISBN 0 340 89900 X

Typeset in Sabon by Hewer Text UK Ltd, Edinburgh
Printed and bound by Mackays of Chatham Ltd, Chatham, Kent

Hodder Headline's policy is to use papers that are natural, renewable and
recyclable products and made from wood grown in sustainable forests. The
logging and manufacturing processes are expected to conform to the
environmental regulations of the country of origin.

Hodder & Stoughton Ltd
A division of Hodder Headline
338 Euston Road
London NW1 3BH

Photographs from the author's collection

For my son Steven,
and his beautiful children Jessica and Joshua

Contents

Acknowledgements

With grateful thanks to Jane Ross-Macdonald, who was able to put this book together from a big pile of documents and a jumble of painful memories; to Katinka Blackford-Newman and her team for their support and vision during the making of the documentary film *A Murder in the Family*; to my publisher Rowena Webb who believed people would want to read my story; to our good friends John and Iris Lawton for their friendship and for always being there with a shoulder to cry on; and to my daughters and all of my family for their dedication and belief. But love and thanks most especially to Alan: without his love, trust and belief in me I could not have endured this journey.

I
Terrible News

On a warm summer's day four years ago my world changed for ever. Everything I had held dear, the little family I had seen grow up and start their own families, my hopes for their futures and dreams for my own – all this was about to be shattered, my universe turned upside down.

Like all terrible days, this one started in an ordinary way. My husband Alan and I had a quiet morning at home in Bingham, a town in Nottinghamshire, and spent the afternoon pottering around in the garden, dead-heading the roses, weeding a little, watering the dried-out pots of geraniums on the patio. We were expecting my daughter Lucy and her son Joseph, and when they arrived I went inside to make a pot of tea while Joseph watched Alan fix part of the fence that had fallen away.

Lucy followed me in, telling me something about what had happened that week at work. Then she stopped, saying she had bad chest pains and would lie down for a while. I also, uncharacteristically, started to feel strange. Sitting next to her on the sofa while she rested with her arms folded protectively over her chest, I suddenly broke out in a cold sweat. At that very moment, in a city thousands of miles away, three men we had never met were taking away something more precious to me than my own life.

The next morning I woke up feeling lethargic and tired although I had gone to bed early the previous evening. Alan was working in the garden again – it was a beautiful day, and

I thought I'd join him. 'Look lively, Margaret – can you grab the end of this hose for me?' he called.

I sat down on a deckchair. 'Sorry, love, I just don't seem to have any energy today.' I sat in the sun for a little, flicking through a magazine but unable to concentrate on it. At about midday I gave in to my exhaustion, saying, 'I think I'll pop in for a nap.' I lay on the sofa, closed my eyes and pulled a wrap over myself. Ah, the sleep of the innocent. Time was running out for me, and someone half a world away was preparing to make the hardest call of his life.

I woke with a jerk. The phone was ringing.

'Is that Margaret Davis?' I could barely hear, the line was very bad.

'Yes. Who is this?' My heart started to thump.

'It's Martin, Steven's friend.' That's strange, what's he phoning me for?

'Yes?' Something bad is coming. I know it.

'It's Steve. He's had an accident.' Bang. A brick on my chest.

'How bad?'

'He's dead, Margaret.' Then the phone cut out.

I looked at the phone. There was something wrong with my hand – it was shaking. In fact my entire body was shaking. I was trying to process what I had just heard and it simply didn't make sense. Inside I was screaming but no sound came out of my mouth. My son. Steven. My son Steven. Steven is dead. My baby. My son. No, it can't be. No. I only spoke to him yesterday. How can this be? I sat on the sofa and buried my face in a cushion. From outside I was aware of the distant clackety sound of the mower and I waited, rigid, for Martin to ring back. This can't be real, it can't. I felt as if I was waiting, powerless to move, for a train to run me over. I must have sat there, totally shut down, for over an hour.

*   *   *

'Who was that on the phone?' Alan appeared by my side. Then: 'What's wrong, Margaret?' He gently took the cushion I was clutching to my face. I stared at him, taking in his sun-weathered face, his torn gardening shirt. Why was he looking so normal? I couldn't reply: if I don't say anything it's not real. Saying the words will make it true. He sat down next to me and took my hands in his. 'Marg, my love. What is it?'

'Steven's dead . . .' I blurted out. 'Steven's dead . . . Steven's dead.' Suddenly it was the only thing I could say, repeating the words like a mantra. I can't remember what Alan said next because the phone rang again – Martin had found a landline. I found my voice.

'What happened, Martin? Tell me, I have to know.' How, what, why, where, who . . .? The questions rushed out of me and I could hear that Steve's friend, a decent guy who I'd met several times, was trying to make it better for me, to tell me things slowly, to let it sink in. But I wanted to know everything, now, all the details – and Martin wasn't going fast enough. I wanted to jump down the phone, I needed to be there, I wanted answers so urgently it hurt.

What I was able to understand was that Steven, my only son, had been sleeping in his bed at home in the Philippines the previous night. Three gunmen burst in, shot Steve several times, then left. Martin, who had been in the next room with his girlfriend, rushed to help him but Steven was already dead.

I was silent for a few moments while I took in this news, my brain working overtime. A tiny worm of a suspicion entered my mind, so small I could not even acknowledge it. So faint, it was no more than a wisp of a thought, and I brushed it away immediately.

'I'll be there in two days,' I said and put the phone down.

'He can't be,' Alan was saying. 'I only spoke to him two

days ago. He can't be dead, not Steven.' He was standing there, saying this over and over again. He must have been in shock.

I had to get to Steven, I had to bring him home, and I had to find out what had happened. And the children. My God, Steven's children! What would happen to them now? I was shivering, and felt Alan wrap a blanket around my shoulders. I knew I was in shock too, I could read the symptoms as well as anyone, But I had to hold off my feelings for now. I couldn't afford to fall apart.

'Are you sure that's the right thing to do, Marg?' Alan said. 'Let's sit and think a while, make some calls. We've both had a shock – let's not rush into anything. What can you achieve by going there?'

'I don't know, but I know I have to go.'

'Well, I'm coming too, then.' He could see my mind was made up. I sat staring at the wall for I don't know how long, but I was aware that Alan was on the phone, booking flights to Manila, the capital city of the Philippines.

'It's done,' he said, his voice unsteady. 'We leave tomorrow afternoon.' Tears were streaming down his face. Dear, kind Alan: he had been Steven's stepfather for fifteen years and loved him as a son. He wrapped me in his arms. 'Oh Marg,' he blurted out. 'Your wonderful boy. What are we to do?'

I looked around the room, focussing on the everyday details that seemed so pointless and tawdry now: a posy of flowers we had picked from the garden yesterday in a vase on the dining table; the remains of our sandwich lunch; bright scatter cushions on the three-piece suite, magazines stacked neatly next to the television. And photographs – oh God, photographs everywhere. Steven as a small blond boy learning to ride his first bike; Steven smiling awkwardly out of a school photo taken when he must have been about

4

eleven; Steven and his two sisters on holiday in Morecambe; Steven graduating; Steven at his marriage to a beautiful Filipina girl. How happy he had been, how normal, how ordinary. And how special. How could he not be alive any more? Who would do this to him? Who could hate him this much? I couldn't bear the pain of imagining him dying, with the knowledge that I hadn't been there to protect him.

First things first, I thought, desperately trying to marshal my thoughts.

'Shall I call Evelyn?' Alan was asking. Evelyn was Steven's wife.

'Yes,' I said. Then I realised he wouldn't be able to.

'No, you can't. I haven't got her mobile phone number, or their house number.' That was true, I always spoke to Steve at work, or on his mobile. Their landline was often not working.

'Well, I expect she'll call you. Poor love is probably in a terrible state.' Yes, she wouldn't have a clue what to do. She did have my number – in fact she'd asked me for it the last time we saw her, as they waved us off at the airport.

'Come on.' I roused myself, feeling that a huge black shroud was just at the edge of my consciousness, nudging at my brain, wanting to envelop me. If I let it take me over I would be lost. I knew I didn't have much time. 'Let's think. We need passports, birth certificates, all the important documents.' I found the box next to my desk where I kept Steven's birth certificate, copies of his marriage certificate, his children's birth certificates, and his will – all of which he had given to me for safekeeping. I knew his bank details as I had invested some of my own money in his new business, so I sent a fax to freeze the account. It was as if I was on autopilot, but the shocking words kept floating through my consciousness. 'Steven's dead . . . Steven's dead.' It didn't make any sense. The words didn't fit together, the phrase wouldn't sit still in my head.

As I was doing this my sister Gillian turned up on the doorstep. She lived opposite us and had been phoned that morning by our brother, who had seen a piece in the *Sun*. It was a small article, but the name leapt out at him: 'Steven Davis, an expat living in the Philippines, was yesterday shot dead by a gunman. Local police are investigating.' Unsure whether to call me – it's not an unusual name after all, and I suppose he didn't want to be the one to break the news to me if I hadn't already heard – he had contacted Gillian to find out if it was our Steve. The moment she entered our house she can have been in no doubt whatsoever that it was, indeed, our Steve. The look on Alan's face as he opened the door said it all.

Wordlessly Gillian hugged me, tears springing to her eyes. She so wanted to help, yet there was nothing anyone could do. Then I remembered my daughters.

'Alan, Gillian – tell the girls, would you?' And together they took on the task of breaking the news to Steve's sisters Lucy and Catherine, and the rest of the family: my three other sisters, my two brothers, a few close friends. I went upstairs, unwilling to hear the words.

I knew that as soon as they heard, the girls would come straight over, but I needed to continue my preparations. Telling myself to think logically, I moved around the house like an automaton, going through the motions but not allowing myself to feel anything. Alan says that now I was in overdrive. I packed my holiday clothes as I had so many times for our regular visits to Steven and his family in the Far East: flowery summer frocks, crush-proof jackets, light tops and skirts, flip-flops and sandals. Somehow they seemed garish and inappropriate, not at all suitable for a mother in mourning. I had no terms of reference for what we were embarking on: I had no idea what would face me, what I was going to do, or what I was going to need. The last thing I packed was a note-book.

It was Gillian who asked me if there was any official help available to someone in this kind of situation. So I phoned the Foreign Office.

'My name is Margaret Davis. I've just heard that my son has been killed in the Philippines.'

A short pause, then: 'Yes, we know about this one. I'm very sorry for your loss.'

They knew about it already?

'What advice can you give me, please?' I asked.

'I can fax you a list of local lawyers who should be able to help you.'

'Oh, yes, all right. I'm flying out tomorrow.' I gave him the fax number.

'When you arrive, make sure you contact one of our staff at the British Consulate there,' and he read out a name and number. 'Good luck.' And that was it.

It didn't occur to me at the time to ask for any more help, or advice, or support. I'm a pretty independent kind of person and I tend to get on with things by myself – so I felt they had provided me with some useful information to get me going. In my naïveté I was quite pleased to have these numbers. It was only much later that I realised I should have been given much more support: I was putting myself and Alan in great danger by rushing off to a foreign country where a family member had just been murdered. Why didn't they warn me? Why didn't they tell me not to go? Why, if they already knew about the case, had no one phoned me? I knew nothing about how investigations were carried out in the Philippines, what the cultural implications were, what to do about talking to the police, how funerals were conducted, what to do about the body. All these things I would have to find out by myself, slowly and painfully and with many false starts. This was my first brush with officialdom and, without realising it, I had already been let down.

The afternoon drifted past. Lucy and Catherine arrived, grief-stricken, staring wildly, asking 'Why? Why?' and crying continually. They needed explanations, just as I did, and I had no answers for them. Much of the day we passed simply sitting in silence at the kitchen table. I could see they weren't sure how to handle me: I was so calm and organised, sorting out all the papers and getting my packing done. All my mother's instincts were focussed on Steven; to my shame I was unable to comfort his sisters yet. One of them went to the bank to withdraw cash from all our accounts to help me in our first few days in the Philippines. Through it all, Alan was our rock, our anchor. He was able to set his own pain aside, hugging us, making tea, trying to make us all feel we would get through this.

I slept fitfully that night, despite having downed several vodkas before going to bed. Not that I was drunk, I just wanted to sleep and I wanted to keep that dark pool of pain at bay. Every time I woke I had just one thought in my mind. 'Why?' 'Why was he killed? Was it a mistake, was it an accident, or was it cold-blooded murder?' In my exhaustion and befuddled state I had the strangest feeling that Steven didn't realise he was dead – that he needed my help to find out what really happened.

Much later I fell into a calmer sleep, and I dreamt about my son. He was calling to me, and I was running towards his voice. I knew he needed me, but I couldn't find him. I glimpsed him in the distance, and ran like mad towards him – but it was that awful slow-motion dream running where you never get anywhere: like Alice in Wonderland. I was running just to stay still. 'Mum, Mum!' came Steven's voice, insistent this time. Finally I caught up with him, but he had his back turned to me. I put out my arms to hug him. When he turned round, he put up his hand to his cheek and his face fell away like a mask, leaving a stranger staring at me.

'Marg, Marg, wake up.' It was Alan with a cup of tea. 'Sorry love, you've been asleep all morning and we ought to get going soon. I've brought you a brew.' I stared at him, unsure for a moment where I was supposed to be going. Then I remembered. Of course this is what it would be like, I knew, each morning of each day that I was to live on this earth without Steven. I would have to re-live every day the fact that he was dead, and I would have to face the day with the knowledge that I would not be speaking to him, texting him, emailing him. That I would never see him again, ever. Even in my dreams, it seemed, he would be lost to me. The thought, and the memory of my dream, left me weak and tearful.

'I don't know if I can do this, Alan,' I confessed. 'I don't think I'm strong enough.'

'Course you can, Margaret. We're together in this, you know – we'll hold each other up and get through it.' Poor Alan, he looked anything but tough that morning, unshaven and half-dressed, his soft blue eyes bloodshot from crying.

'But Steven never did anything bad to anyone: nobody deserves that kind of end. It doesn't make sense.' I knew I had to go, there would be lots for me to do, even if it was only helping Evelyn by taking care of the children for a while. 'Evelyn won't know what to do, and the children will be so confused. Poor little mites.' I knew I had to get to the children.

That morning Martin phoned again – he had promised to call to discuss plans for meeting up.

'I was thinking of going to Makati from the airport,' I said. 'Can you meet us there?' Makati was the business district of Manila, where Steven had rented a house – the house where he had been killed.

'Don't do that. Get in a cab and come straight to Angeles.' Angeles was where Steve owned a house, and to where he returned at the weekends to be with his family. It was a three-hour drive from Manila.

'Oh, all right. Why?'

'I'll tell you when we meet. In the meantime, don't talk to anyone, keep your head down, and meet me in the lobby of the Oasis Hotel.' His voice was staccato, urgent. I shivered, feeling the hand of fear on my heart. What could he mean?

I don't remember the three-hour journey to the airport but I do remember suddenly finding myself at the check-in desk. It was horribly familiar. How often had I stood on this very spot, excited at the thought of seeing Steven, looking forward to the prospect of several weeks with him, Ev and the kids. But this was all wrong: we never went to the Philippines in July. How could this be happening? A queue of people stood in front of me, clearly in holiday mood, and the check-in girl looked unbearably cheerful as she flicked through passports and handed out boarding passes. We were not part of this holiday scene, we were marked. I felt myself falling as my legs buckled under me. Then Alan was there, holding me, talking to me softly, leading me aside to a plastic chair. I made no sound but the tears came then, fiercely and painfully, silent sobs racking my body. I'm a bit asthmatic, and I think I was hyperventilating. People were watching, pointing, but I didn't care – and then we were surrounded by ground staff and ushered without fuss into a private lounge.

'Come on old girl,' Alan said, managing a smile. 'This is for Steven. You can do it.'

The seventeen-hour flight that followed was one of the worst experiences of my life. Aeroplanes are places where emotion is always controlled – you may be terrified of flying, but you don't let on. Turbulence may disturb you but you merely grip the arm-rests or shrug stoically at your neighbour. You sit next to strangers for hours and rarely give away any personal information. The air hostesses are beautiful and unruffled, acting as if it is normal to be handing out warm towels and champagne 37,000 feet up in the sky. But what are you supposed to do if your son has just been killed? Smile and be civilised, exchange idle chit-chat, pretend to be going on holiday? Having held myself together over the past two days while we prepared for this trip, the grief that had unleashed itself in the check-in lounge could be restrained no longer. I had nothing to distract my thoughts, and like a hideous film on a loop the imagined images of Steven's last moments played themselves over and over in my mind. In vain did Alan try to coax me to watch a film, or eat – in fact even the sight of a chocolate bar placed on the plastic tray before me was unbearable. It was Steve's favourite brand. I felt empty, sick, utterly bereft. Alan was solicitous, trying to help, handing me tissues and shielding me from the curious glances of passengers as they passed up and down the aisles. He never let go of my hand the whole while. The hours slid slowly by, and it seemed as if we would never get there. I almost wished we never would, that the plane would crash and wipe out my pain, taking me swiftly to Steven.

Night fell and I looked out into the deepening blackness. It seemed that this was what my world had become. A dark and lonely place devoid of meaning. The plane's engines droned on, and up here in the anonymous blackness I felt as if I had fallen through a chink in time, caught between life as it had been and life as it would be. A face, swollen with crying, looked back at me from the tiny window: it hardly looked like me. If I wasn't Steven's mother any more, who was I?

*   *   *

Steven was my first child, born 27 March 1970. His father was Joe, who worked as a maintenance fitter at Butlins holiday camp in Skegness – which was where we met when I was on holiday there with my mum and dad. We were still kids at the time, really: I was seventeen and he was nineteen. We moved into a little rented flat by the sea, and although we never had much money, I enjoyed bringing up our little family. After Steve came two girls, Catherine and Lucy. I worked at night to pass a social-work management degree, and once the children were all at school I got myself a management position in a home for the elderly not far from where we lived. Joe and I got married in 1979 and we moved to a bigger house in Nottingham. Life was good, but one day everything changed. How quickly life's reverses come! Two days before Steven's fourteenth birthday Joe was injured in a motorbike accident that left him brain-damaged for two years before he died. For the first few months, while he was on life support, I used to go to the hospital in the early evening and stay with him until the morning. I switched to working part-time and spent as much time at home with the kids as I was able to. But the children were amazing: Steven drew up a chore rota which they all stuck to, and the usual teenage arguments all but disappeared. He did the garden and the girls helped me take care of the house. I saw so many parents during that time at the hospital who lost young sons and daughters to illness and accident, I often had cause to thank my lucky stars my three were healthy. I'll never forget, on the day Joe finally died, Steven saying to me, 'I'm the man of the family now, Mum. You can rely on me.' He was as good as his word, and helped me through those difficult first months as a depleted family. Together we learnt the skills of survival, resilience, and the importance of supporting each other. I sometimes wonder if my determination to survive catastrophe was moulded by those early years.

A few years later I got together with Alan – a former workmate of Joe's – and he was very quickly welcomed into the family by my three children. Although we were only in our thirties we decided not to have any more children, and Alan was more than happy to be a stepdad to my three. He was never heavy-handed or distant, always solid and dependable, taking his lead from me on how I wanted them brought up. They grew to love and trust him, and I know how fortunate I have been in finding someone like Alan. I don't think I would have been able to get through the past few years without him. We have been to hell and back together.

As a little boy Steven was mischievous, and enjoyed clowning around at school. I remember after his first day at school I asked the teacher how he'd got on. 'Oh, he'll be fine,' she said, 'as long as he stops trying to make the other children laugh.' As he grew up he quietened down – perhaps as a result of his dad's death. He became studious rather than sporty, not one of those tearaway lads always out on bikes, playing truant or always cheeking their parents. I was proud of his sensible attitude, his caring ways with his younger sisters, and the way he would pay attention to his school work. He and I were very close, partly I think because of the loss of his first dad, but also because he was a naturally loving, friendly boy. He didn't keep secrets from me as I think his sisters did, we were always able to talk about everything. As he grew older he showed considerable flair at the computer, and when he left college he got a job developing programmes and writing software – he was still living at home and spent hours tapping away in front of his screen. Sometimes I would worry that he didn't go out more – young men ought to be spending lots of time with their mates, going out with girls, going to pubs, clubs and gigs. I wondered if he had spent so much time trying to be a good boy for me that he had become too much of a homebody. But Steven didn't seem interested: 'I'm happy as I am, Mum,' he used to claim. 'Stop fussing!' But he did join the local army cadets and a youth club, both of which led to various social and fundraising activities, and he and Alan used to go speed driving together. Eventually he did meet a girl, a nineteen-year-old student, and they soon became engaged. She was more interested in going to parties than in work, and when they inevitably split up Steven was heartbroken.

So it was that when he was offered a lucrative job with an IT company in Hong Kong, I encouraged him to take it. He was only twenty-one, but I knew it would provide a new focus for him, would help him get over the girlfriend, and would represent a fine challenge in a new environment. Like any mother I was sad, knowing he was leaving the nest – but I told myself that this was what parenting was all about: helping your children towards the courage and independence of spirit that would lead them to make positive choices for themselves. If only Hong Kong wasn't so far away! 'Don't worry,' he would say, 'I can always find my way home.' After we had said our tearful goodbyes at the airport, I went to the observation deck to watch his plane take off and soar up into the sky until it was no more than a tiny speck, wondering what his new life would hold for him. I cried all the way home. Of course I feel guilty now, knowing I had encouraged him so much to go. How I wish now I could turn back the clock.

It was in Hong Kong that he settled first, living the high life with his young friends. He was shocked at how expensive it all was, but excited to be independent and living somewhere different and energetic. He lived in a tiny flat about fifty floors up, and spent all his money on socialising. He was working on the new airport, installing computers and working out the software – quite a big, complex job, and he was one of the project managers. To relax, he and his friends would spend weekends on junks – Chinese-style boats – visiting the outlying islands to swim and dive. Sometimes they would spend a day or so in the Philippines, which was only a short flight away, a popular destination for people seeking nightlife and beaches. It was there that he met a young Filipina woman and fell in love. They were so happy, and even invited us to join them on their honeymoon: how thrilled and honoured we were. After their wedding they moved to Angeles City in the Philippines, where they had two children and Steven set up his own software company.

He worked really hard, sometimes twenty-hour days – when we logged on to the internet in the morning he'd often be there, still online. He was wealthy, certainly compared with his contemporaries back in England, and appeared to be leading an exciting, interesting life in this very different culture. He knew how proud I was of him, both for his courage in making a new life in a different country, and for getting married and settling down before he started a family. Alan and I spent several months of each year staying with Steven and his young family, and we had been planning to buy a plot of land and build our own house there.

Like Steven's life, these dreams were now over.

As the plane started its descent I looked down onto this foreign land of dense, polluted cities, vast open scrubland, dark jungles and jewel-like islands. This country so full of contradictions, that had at times enchanted and at others enraged Steven; this country that had claimed my son's heart – and now his life. It was waiting for me.

Somewhere down there were the answers I was seeking.

2

The Funeral Parlour

We knew the drill well. Step off the plane. Get into rickety bus to go to airport building. Try to find trolley that probably won't work while waiting ages for luggage to be hand-loaded from plane to carousel. Fend off all the local porters anxious for a few coins by carrying bags, make way through immigration. Look for Steven grinning and waving in the arrivals hall. Of course I knew logically that he would not be there, but still I scanned the waiting white faces, hoping like a mad fool that there had been some mistake, a practical joke – and there he would be as usual. I think this was where it started to feel truly wrong, out of joint. This was his city, we had come to see him, and he was gone.

Emerging from the air-conditioned airport to join the taxi queue, we were hit by a stifling blast of hot air, full of the strange smells of this country – diesel fumes mixed with something sweet and unfamiliar. It was a smell that for me had always been associated with the anticipation of several weeks' holiday with my adored son. Now, inhaling it made me feel nauseous. No longer enticingly exotic, it seemed instead dirty, putrid: there was something rotten in the air.

We endured the three-hour drive to Angeles City in silence, both of us fearful of what lay ahead. The car was old, and the driver was smoking. I had never minded the uncomfortable journey before: after all, we were used to being picked up by Steven in his beaten-up old Kia – he used to laugh about it, saying, 'It gets me from A to B, so why worry? I don't want to set myself apart as a rich Westerner with a flash car – this does the job for me.'

That was Steve all over – he was very aware of the discrepancy in wealth between him and the locals he worked with and lived amongst. It always struck me how accepting he was that it was his responsibility to give something back to the people. He was incredibly generous with his money – always giving gifts and helping his wife's family, who lived on a poverty-stricken island in a remote corner of the country. He had bought them a water-purifying system, a generator, medicine and food – even a boat to help them fish for their livelihood. He believed that if you give a man a meal he'll eat it, but if you give a man the means to fish he will be able to feed his family for ever. It was well known in the Philippines that if you marry a local girl you take on responsibility for the family, and Steven was happy to do this. Fortunate for them that their daughter had found Steven. It was on one of his weekend trips to Manila with his friends for diving, fishing and partying that he met Evelyn, a pretty young dancer working in one of the bars. Steven fell for her instantly. He sent us email pictures of her, loads of them: he was really smitten. I must admit, when we met her I remember thinking that she wasn't quite the sort of girl I'd have chosen for him – she was very young and totally uneducated – but I was won over like him by her politeness, her ready smile and her respectful attitude. And so beautiful! White teeth, flawless skin, shiny black hair: we decided she was a lovely little thing. When he announced their engagement I was delighted. 'I'm rescuing her, Mum,' he had said proudly.

The journey seemed to be taking forever. I looked at my watch: it was late afternoon and I had eaten hardly anything. Perhaps I'd be able to force myself to eat something at the hotel – I realised I needed to keep my strength up, but the very thought of food made me feel ill. I wondered if Martin would be expecting us to go out for a meal. He was a nice guy, was Martin – a Canadian who had set up the software business with Steve about two years earlier. Full of jokes and fun, Martin also had a serious, kind side. We had often seen him at the offices.

By the time we got to Angeles it was early evening. Dusk was falling, and with it the intense heat of the day subsided. It never gets cool in the Philippines, though, and walking towards the entrance of the hotel we were hit again by a wave of warm, sickly air. I felt Alan's steadying arm in the small of my back guiding me inside, and we scanned the lobby for a familiar face. Three of Steve's colleagues immediately came forward to greet us: Martin, Brian and another Steven – a friend of his from his flying club. There was also a Filipino guy we had never seen before. I guessed he was a security guard. Their faces were kind, but I could see pity and something like fear in their eyes. Martin in particular kept looking about nervously. We checked in, and left our bags to be carried up to the room later. Without saying much, the four men led us to the lifts and up into one of the rooms. The guard stayed outside the room.

We sat down and Martin poured us all glasses of water, his hand a little unsteady. He apologised for having been the one to give me such bad news two days earlier – already it seemed like a lifetime away. He was talking so fast we could hardly catch what he was saying: he was in a dreadful state. I realised he needed reassurance and I put my hand over his. 'It's a very hard thing to do, I know. I've lost a son, and you've lost a good friend. You were quite right to phone me, and I am grateful for your support today. We have come here because it seemed like the right thing to do, but we are not quite sure what we ought to be doing. First, if you can, could you please tell us exactly what happened that night?'

Martin composed himself and began. 'Of course. I'll tell you everything I know. Steve and I had both spent last weekend working in the office here in Angeles. On Monday we drove to the main Makati office as usual, and worked non-stop until Wednesday, when we were both exhausted. We decided to rent a DVD and get some take-out pizzas to eat at the house in Makati where the two of us stay during the week. Steve went to bed at about 11 pm and I went to the airport to pick up my girlfriend Jennifer, who was coming over from Hong Kong on business.'

I sat staring at Martin, drinking in the words. These were the last hours my precious son spent alive – I had to know everything.

'We came back at about 2 am.' He stopped to pour himself a large shot of whisky – I could see it was taking its toll on him, having to recount the grisly story.

'OK Martin, take your time,' I murmured.

'Jennifer and I had just gone to bed, around 2.15 am, when two Filipino guys burst into the room. They were waving guns and were holding cushions over their faces so I could not see them. Then one of them, the smaller one, shouted "Move!", waving his gun and torch at me. I could feel Jennifer's whole body freeze. They shoved the gun at her and told her to get up, so she wrapped the sheet around herself and they pushed her into the bathroom. They hissed at her to be quiet, then they demanded my wallet and car keys.'

'You must have been terrified,' said Alan, voicing what we were all thinking.

'I thought I was going to die. I was sitting in my bed naked, I had my hands up, I was shaking, begging them not to kill me. I just couldn't stop shivering. I'm ashamed that I didn't even think of Steven, I just didn't want to die.

'Then the bigger guy forced me to stand up, which I could

barely do – my legs were like jelly. He said to a third guy, "*Ito ba? Ito ba?* Is this him, is this him?" The third guy said, "No, no," sounding panicked, and they pushed me back into bed and told me to stay quiet. A moment later we heard one of them say, "In here, now, quick!" and two shots rang out. Then two more. Suddenly there was dead silence, then we heard them say, "Go, go," and then they were gone – they left the way they had come in, through the front door.'

'They came in through the front door? How did they do that? What happened next? Did you go to find Steve?' I didn't want to sound accusing; I just wanted to know that he wasn't left to bleed to death alone.

'When we dared to – remember we were in shock and we were half-expecting the men to come back to finish us off – I let Jennifer out of the bathroom and we dashed to Steve's room. There was blood all over the place, and Steve . . .' Here his voice broke. There were tears in his eyes, which we wiped roughly away. 'Steve was just lying staring up at the ceiling, not moving. I thought he was in shock, so I tried to give him CPR and Jen rushed out into the street to call for help. But I realised he was gone. When the paramedics arrived they pronounced him dead at the scene.'

My mind was racing as he told me all this. A terrible aching sadness for my poor Steven, exhausted after several days' hard work, sleeping peacefully in his own bed. I remembered tucking him up as a child, and how he loved the comfort and security of clean sheets and a soft pillow. Fierce anger, too, that he had had no way of defending himself: I imagined him waking up, and realising in a split second that he was going to die. Was there a struggle? I wondered if he had cried out, if he had recognised any of the men, I wondered what his last thoughts were of: his two beautiful children, his wife, perhaps his mother? Then logic kicked in. I knew there was a question I had to ask.

'How do you think they got in?'

'They could have picked the lock, I suppose, but Steven said last week that he'd lost his house keys. I was going to get my set copied for him – I think he assumed his kids had been playing with them. He could have dropped them at work, I guess. Or anywhere.'

Lost his house keys? This sounded suspicious.

'Were there any problems at work, anyone you can think of who might have had a grudge against him?' said Alan. 'It sounds to me as if it could have something to do with a business deal that went wrong.'

'Rubbish, Steven didn't have any enemies,' I cut in.

'I know,' said Martin. 'I've been racking my brains about that one, but I just can't think of anyone. He was so popular; all the staff are devastated. They used to call him "Sir Steve", he was such a gentleman. I can't think of any deals that had gone sour, or any shady characters we were doing business with. We're pretty careful.'

We all sat in silence for several moments, absorbing the horror.

'What about the police? Did they arrive?' I asked eventually.

'Oh yes, and they took us both in for questioning, we were suspects at first – and for all I know, we still are. So they took fingerprints and so on. I was in no fit state to be questioned, but Jennifer was more useful. She's a Filipina so she had understood all the Tagalog the gunmen were speaking. The next day we both went to the station and gave statements. I tried to describe one of the men I had seen so that a photofit picture could be drawn up.'

'Money is a big motivator over here – can you think of anyone he owed money to?' asked Alan.

'Steve? No, he was incredibly honourable, as you know. I did know that his ATM card wasn't working that day – he'd tried to get money out for the pizza and I ended up buying them both because his card wasn't accepted.' He smiled ruefully. 'At least I was able to buy him his last meal.'

'Have you spoken to Evelyn?' I asked, wondering how she was coping in all this mess. She still hadn't called me, which was odd, but we really should go and see her at once.

'I tried to call her the morning after Steve was killed, but there was no answer.' He paused, then continued. 'Margaret, I've got to say that Steve and Evelyn had not been getting on too well recently – there were household bills that hadn't been paid and he was worried that there wasn't enough food in the house for Jessica and Joshua. I don't feel comfortable saying this, but I feel she may know something . . .'

His words hit home.

'Don't be ridiculous!' burst out Alan. 'Evelyn may be ignorant, she may be arrogant even, but she isn't a criminal. She'd never have anything to do with something like this. We know she had been lending money to her relatives, and we know Steve understood that. Surely you can't be suggesting . . .'

'No, no.' Martin backed off. 'Look – I don't know what to think. I do think Steve was unhappy about something at home, though.'

'If the police are doing their job they'll find out what happened,' I said, 'and I'm going to go and see them myself as soon as I can.' Martin's words had struck a chord with me. I knew Steve had been having problems with Evelyn, and the tiny seed of doubt that had entered my mind the moment I heard he was dead started to germinate. I needed to think.

We then discussed what to do the next day. The first awful duty was to go to the funeral parlour, three hours' drive away. Martin had discovered from officials at the morgue in Makati that after Steven had been identified his body was released by the police and sent to the funeral home in

Angeles, presumably at Evelyn's request. Brian offered to pick us up and drive us there: they all felt we should not leave the hotel without an escort. After that we planned to go to Steve's home and see what we could do to help.

As the three concerned friends and their silent minder left, Brian – who had lived in the Philippines for many years – advised, 'I don't want to scare you, but I feel I ought to warn you to be careful. If someone had a reason to kill Steven, that someone might also have a reason to kill Steven's parents. Whoever stood to gain from his death may feel you are in the way. If you need to go anywhere just give me a call and I'll come and get you.'

We sat up late that night, feeling as if we were in a kind of limbo. We were emotionally exhausted, but not physically tired because of course our bodies were still in a different time zone. I couldn't forget what Martin had said about Evelyn, and I wanted to talk to Alan about what it might mean. But he wouldn't be drawn. 'Give it a rest, Margaret. We've only just got here: don't go leaping to conclusions. Ev's not a bad person. Do you really think she'd do that to her children's dad? This is something to do with business, you mark my words.'

I lay awake that night replaying my last conversation with Steven two days before he died. Various items had been going missing in the house, the electricity had been cut off, and he thought Evelyn had been pawning jewellery. For months she had been diverting household money in other directions, and when asked to explain she would blame a sick auntie, impoverished parents, a pregnant sister, a cousin in trouble – there was always some family member in need of Steven's largesse. He had been so generous for so many years, but his patience was being sorely tried. He had told me he was going to cut off her allowance if this didn't stop, but he also talked about moving with her to another part of town away from her relatives. He'd even talked about divorce, but I hadn't taken him seriously. Was it possible Evelyn could be involved? Surely not.

The next day dawned hot, overcast and humid. I was hungry but feeling sick, and just managed to swallow a cup of coffee and half a piece of toast before Brian arrived to drive us to the funeral parlour. It was on the outskirts of Angeles City on the edge of a busy highway. 'Galang Funeral Home Chapel' it proclaimed in tall red letters above an open doorway. A stack of coffins piled higgledy-piggledy on top of each other stood at the entrance of the building. To the left of the doorway people were selling ice cream and frying food; women were washing clothes in large metal bowls, collecting water from a pipe on the side of the road. This was typical of this country, I thought. Death is allowed no dignity or solemnity: life in its messiness and cheapness rushes past, while human tragedy passes unnoticed and unmarked. Not by me, I thought defiantly. I held my head up, knowing that I was being watched as I entered the funeral home. They all knew a white European was lying in a casket inside.

'Nana here, Nana here!' A small dark-haired child hurled herself at me. It was Jessica, Steven's three-year-old daughter. I picked her up and hugged her tightly, tears pricking my eyes. How much did she know of what had happened, I wondered. She was so little, so trusting. Looking around the room at the caskets, I immediately saw which one must be Steven's: it was white with a glass top, surrounded by large displays of flowers. I wanted to rush away then, to escape from this place of death. Perhaps I thought that by running away I could stop time; that I would never have to see what lay in the coffin. Alan scooped up Jessie and I walked over to it, full of trepidation. I looked down, and there within the white silken lining was Steven. Dear God, here was my son. I could hardly breathe.

He looked as if he was asleep, but with a pale, unshaven, empty face that showed me that he was, unarguably, dead. I was shocked to see him looking so normal, so untouched by the bullets, and yet so completely absent. Wake up, I prayed silently. Wake up. *Wake up*. My whole soul cried out to him. Steven, my first child, I brought you into the world, I nurtured you, I watched you grow from a little tacker into a fine lad, a decent and kind young man, and a proud father. You were my support and I yours. Our lives were so entwined and now we are separated for ever. How cruel it is to see a dead child, how contrary to all the laws of nature that a son should die before a mother. He was only thirty-two. I wanted to touch him, to cradle him in my arms, breathe life back into his cold, stiff body. I remembered the last time I saw him, back in March as we said our sad goodbyes after a three-month visit. 'You'll soon be back, Mum,' he had said, grinning. How painfully right he was. I thought of how Evelyn had stood back at the time, thoughtfully watching us bid farewell to each other. She wasn't normally there to see us off, and I remember thinking at the time it was a little strange. This was when she had asked me for my number, saying, 'In case I need to call you.'

Just one more hour, I prayed. What I would give for just one more hour with him.

I was brought back to earth by Jessie voicing exactly my thoughts. She was leaning over the coffin and banging on the glass top. 'Wake up, Daddy. Nana's here now, you can wake up!' She looked up at me expectantly, needing the kind of attention that I wasn't able to give just then. This wasn't a suitable place for a child. Turning round to look for her mother, I spotted Evelyn sitting in a pew, by herself, looking beautiful and tragic. A black scarf draped around her head, a black suit and dark glasses. She did not rise when she saw me. I went to sit next to her.

'How are you, Evelyn?' She did not reply, merely shook her head. Was she being rude, or tactful? But of course, she was still in shock. My heart went out to her.

'I'm so sorry, Evelyn. This must be as terrible for you as it is for us. We just cannot believe it.' Again, no reply, just a nod. She held her handkerchief up to her face. I needed to keep trying – it was important to reach out to this girl. I knew her very well, after all, and we had always treated her like our own daughter. When we had first met her we had been shocked at how young she seemed, but she was so attractive: delicate Asian features, deep brown eyes, a winning smile – and over the years we had become used to her slightly odd ways, believing our job was to support Steve in the choice he had made. Perhaps it was seeing her sitting there in a smart black suit that reminded me of the day of their wedding, when she wore a similar suit of white silk. Their best man Ralph had said something strange that day: 'He could do much better.' I had assumed he was jealous, but now, as I sat next to her, his words came back to me with prophetic resonance: 'Steve's making a big mistake.'

Nevertheless, I knew Steve would want me to be kind to her now.

'We want to help, Evelyn. This is a difficult time for you. Have you spoken to the police? Do they know anything?'

Still no answer came, no greeting, no condolences. We sat in silence for a time. Then something occurred to me. 'I think it is rather unusual for the body to be laid out so soon, shouldn't they be doing tests or something? He died less than three days ago in Makati and now here he is in a coffin in Angeles. Do you know why?' At this she mumbled something about wanting him nearer home. I didn't want her to feel I was questioning her, so I moved back to the coffin, feeling her watching me from behind.

I wanted to remember everything about my son. His hair was brushed back a little further than he would normally have worn it, and his fists were clenched. I could see where he had bitten his nails down to the quick – a nervous habit he'd held onto since childhood. He was dressed in a white shirt, tie and suit – definitely not his: he never owned a suit. If I closed my eyes a little perhaps I could believe it wasn't really him. After a while Evelyn joined me, and I held her hand as we stood looking down at her husband. I glanced at the names on the cards: they were from the girls at the office, Angeles City Flying Club, the Roadhouse Bar. None from Evelyn or any of her family. Was this normal? Perhaps it was a cultural thing.

'Have you seen Martin?' she asked suddenly. Her voice was a little too loud: she sounded nervous. I couldn't see her eyes, and something told me to play safe.

'Why?'

'He was there, Ma'am.' She had always called me this – it was a mark of respect used by the locals towards Western women. The way she pronounced it, it sounded like 'Mum'.

'I thinking he maybe recognise the killer. The men in the house for twenty minutes, Ma'am, I think Martin maybe see the man who do this thing.' *Dis ting.* Her pidgin English used to be endearing; now it grated. It was the sound of the country that had taken my son.

Hang on. How did she know they were in the house for twenty minutes? Had she been told this by the police? Why was she so keen to know if Martin had recognised anyone? Well, we all surely wanted to know who did it. Yet still I felt I ought to play my cards close to my chest – if Evelyn knew something, I mustn't let her know I suspected anything. I'd try to get her to drop her defences.

'I haven't seen Martin yet Ev, all I know is that my son has been murdered and I don't know how or why.' I put my arms around her. 'We're in this together, we're on the same side. The most important thing is to make sure the children are OK.' It would have been nice if she'd asked me how I was feeling – after all, Steven was my son. In her situation most wives would be begging for help, fearful for their future and their children's future. I could hear Jessica outside with Alan, chatting as they bought ice cream.

'Where is Joshua?' I asked.

'He is teething,' she answered. 'I leave him with the maid.'

'What about you, have you got enough money?' I asked, knowing full well what the answer would be.

'No Ma'am, I have nothing. I cannot get money from bank and I must buy food and things for the kids. My landlady, she want me to move out, she not happy with me now.'

I gave her some cash, reassured her that it would be all right, and said I would see her again soon, and that I wanted to spend some time with Jessica and her little brother Joshua, who was just a baby. She took the money eagerly, and again I told myself not to dwell on what Martin had said. I had to believe she knew nothing about this, I had to trust that she was innocent: she was the mother of Steven's beloved children. Yet something was bothering me. Something wasn't right. I determined to make some notes when I got back to the hotel.

But when we reached the safety of our room all I could do was lie in Alan's arms and weep. The shock and grief of seeing my dead son, and the strain of trying to stay in control, overwhelmed me. I was crushed, broken, and I felt that I would never, ever be whole again.

Over the next few days I went to see Steven several times. I wanted to gaze upon his face and think about the happy times. And there had been many: he dearly loved this country, and he had welcomed us into his home for months on end over the past few years. We had visited perfect sun-bleached tropical islands, we had learnt how to dive together; we had even been microlight-flying with him. One memorable time I got into difficulties deep under water: I think I'd lost my flipper, and suddenly I was having trouble breathing. Steven dragged me to the top and started doing first aid on me. It was funny at the time, but now I think he probably saved my life. I remembered Evelyn saying, 'Steve always happy when he with his mother.' *Mudder.* The best time of all was when Catherine and Lucy and their children came with us for a holiday to mark the millennium. The girls and Evelyn used to go out of an evening, leaving us oldies to sit enjoying the balmy night air – they were like three giggly sisters. Evelyn was shy at first, and so different from my girls, but they gossiped together about babies and clothes, and I knew Steve was thrilled to see them getting on so well. Jessie was a baby and delighted in her big-boy cousins Jack and Joseph. What a treat for an ordinary family from the Midlands. Everything seemed perfect. How had this idyllic lifestyle suddenly crashed around us? Surely, surely Evelyn wouldn't have wanted it to end?

I kept calling Evelyn that week, asking her if I could come to the house to see the children. Each time she had an excuse: her parents and sisters were there, she was too busy, or the children were playing with friends. One evening when I called the house Jessica answered the phone excitedly, saying, 'I am eating chicken, Nana!' I could hear what sounded like the noise of a party – music and laughter. Evelyn herself sounded very happy – perhaps drunk, perhaps on drugs. She admitted that she was having a wake for Steven with friends and family, and they were eating the food she had bought with my money. 'It is my custom,' she said. I accepted that this was perhaps a cultural thing, but I felt shocked and upset that she had not thought to include me and Alan. There she was having a high old time, and we were just sitting there.

Unsure about how to behave in this country, and confused about what I should be doing, I called a contact in England. He was a local town councillor in Nottingham (I had helped him campaign for office, as I had been a councillor too) and, usefully I thought, was also a lawyer. We both knew our MP very well. It was Ken Clarke. Yes, that Ken Clarke, the famous fat one who wanted to be Tory leader. I was sure that between them they were bound to be able to help. I asked him what the procedure for dealing with a death of a relative in a foreign country was, and – more importantly – what I should do to help my grandchildren. I was worried that Evelyn seemed to be neglecting them, had very little money, and was being evicted from her home. Would it be possible to take them to the UK for a holiday while things settled down here? He promised to try to find out some information for me, and I felt reassured.

That week I also paid a visit to Evelyn's landlady, who lived in the same block as her. I had met her before, when Steve had asked me to sort out the rent that had mysteriously not been paid as Evelyn had claimed. What I heard made me very concerned. 'That house is full of noisy people, Ma'am. Parties all the time, alcohol and drugs I think. Mr Steve he go to Makati and the wife she have too many friends. Many men. My other tenants they not happy.' I offered to pay her a year's rent in advance: the children needed somewhere decent to live, and if they could not stay here I feared they would go to live with relatives hundreds of miles away. The landlady refused, and I started to realise a little of what my son had been dealing with. Poor Steve, no wonder he was angry with Evelyn – his house was overrun with strangers when he wasn't there. I did not like what I heard, and I was deeply concerned about these men, whoever they were. And what of the children while all this was going on? Were they just left with the maids?

One evening we left the hotel for a stroll around the city. I knew we were going against Brian's advice, but I was going crazy cooped up in our room. We walked and walked, barely noticing our surroundings, just wanting to banish the vision of poor, pale, dead Steven. Without realising it, we found ourselves outside the very bar where Steven and Evelyn had first met. We'd been in many times over the past few years – it was a favourite haunt of ours, and we knew several of the girls who worked there. They used to call Steve 'The Computer' because he'd go there to work or chat to his mates: he was never interested in the girls.

'Come on, Marg, we could do with a drink,' said Alan. He was right. As soon as we sat down the proprietor came over with drinks on the house.

'I am so sorry for your loss. Steven was a good man.' If we had thought we could escape our grief by leaving the hotel we were wrong, but at least the man was being kind, and we felt close to Steven by sitting at his usual table. Alan and I took refuge in talking about the past. He reminded me that when we first heard that Steve had met a girl who worked in a bar we had imagined her pulling pints like the barmaids in our local pub. We were glad he'd met someone who would help him forget his former fiancée, but Evelyn was weak and ill and he had taken her to buy medicine – it took her several months to recover. Evelyn became Steve's pet project, and he started lavishing money on her, buying her jewellery, clothes, shoes and presents, and taking her family gifts. 'He spoilt her rotten,' remarked Alan.

'If only he'd settled down in England with an ordinary girl like Lucy or Catherine,' I said, not for the first time.

'Yes, someone who would have supported him in his job and been proud of his achievements. She wouldn't ever say

how well he was doing at work. Never.' Alan had always
been upset about Evelyn's lack of interest in Steve's job.

'He loved her to bits. We had to support his choice, didn't
we?' I said.

'Yes, he saw beyond her faults. He loved her, he was a very
loyal boy.'

'Well, at the end of the day you have to leave your kids to
live their own lives.'

It wasn't pints she had been pulling, of course, it was
men. Like many other girls from the impoverished outer
islands of the Philippines, she had come to the big city to
seek work and to make her fortune. Angeles, perhaps more
than other cities, had a thriving sex industry due to the
American airbase that used to be there. These girls have
one primary goal – understandable when you see where
they come from – to find a wealthy Western husband.
Wages in the bars are horrifyingly low, as little as 130 pesos
per day (the equivalent of £1.20), but the girls are expected
to supplement this by selling sexual favours to foreign
businessmen. Most make do with elderly has-beens; how
lucky Evelyn was to find young, handsome Steven. Girls as
young as twelve worked as dancers in these bars, and they
had the world-weary look of old pros. No wonder Evelyn
had been on antibiotics for so long. And no wonder Steven
wanted to rescue her: these girls must have to close down a
part of their soul just to survive.

The bar was filling up and the music was starting. Someone came and sat at our table and struck up a conversation
with us. As is often the way with strangers, we ended up
sharing our story with him, and told him about our son and
daughter-in-law.

'It's a well-known fact,' declared the stranger – who was
somewhat the worse for wear – 'You can take the girl from
the bar but you can't take the bar from the girl.' How I hoped

he was not right. At that moment a group of girls dressed in bikinis sashayed onto the stage: it was time for us to leave.

'If Steve had a fault,' said Alan as we wandered back to the hotel, 'I would say that he was too trusting.'

'They're very loving, these Filipina girls. They can be very persuasive. I think he just fell for the whole thing, hook, line and sinker.' I'd had a few drinks myself and was starting to feel aggressive.

'Yes, perhaps he thought that if he gave her everything she wanted she would become everything he wanted her to be. Nothing was too good for her.'

Now that I thought about it, how extraordinary it must have felt for Evelyn to go from earning a pound a day in the bar to running a household with a thousand pounds a month. It must have blown her mind.

I continued to call Evelyn, leaving messages several times a day. She eventually called back and asked if I could meet her late that night in a bar that I knew to be in a disreputable district. Something told me not to go – what a strange time and place to want to meet me! I pleaded tiredness, and eventually she agreed to meet me at the funeral parlour one afternoon.

I took Brian along, and on the way there he told me he had heard from colleagues at work that Evelyn had been on the radio the previous day, appealing for legal advice: she was hoping for someone to help her with a claim against the business for Steven's shares. She had been informed that I was Steven's beneficiary (it was something he had set up years ago when I gave him a loan for his business) and that if she wanted money she would have to come to me. That can't have pleased her much, I thought.

Together we stood beside Steven, who looked so at rest in his casket.

'This is most expensive casket, Ma'am. I wanted to have

the best for Steven.' She pronounced his name 'Stayban', looking at me for approval. Was it that she was naïvely eager to please? Or were these the actions of a guilty child keen to curry favour? Then she asked me about Martin again, and what he saw. I shrugged.

'What do *you* think happened, Evelyn?'

'Me Ma'am? I don't know. Me and Steven, we were very happy, last weekend we had fun with the kids and then Steven kiss me before he went to Makati. First thing I know the police call me.'

Then she dropped a bombshell: 'I am pregnant, Ma'am. Eight weeks.'

I swallowed hard. 'Did Steven know?'

'No, I was going to tell him this weekend and have a celebration. Steven loves kids, he wanted more.' Really? I thought. He had told me he wouldn't have any more children until things were easier at home. I wondered if they had had a night of reconciliation.

'Evelyn, love, I think it's best not to have this baby – you have Jessie and Josh, and you must look after them.' The words left my mouth almost before I was aware of them. What was I thinking? I loved children, but we were now entering dark, unfamiliar territory. Their father dead, my one driving urge was to protect Jessie and Josh – and I couldn't banish a gnawing sense of doubt about their mother.

'No,' she replied hotly. 'This is a special baby. It must stay in my body.'

I changed the subject, knowing that the funeral was arranged for the following day.

'We need to talk about tomorrow. What arrangements have you made? I'd really like to take Steven back to England to be cremated. It is what he would have wanted.' She was silent for a moment. Then she shook her head.

'He must be buried here in my country,' she replied. I couldn't see her face as she was still wearing those blasted sunglasses. Was she manipulating me, or was she following her Catholic traditions? I tried without success to get her to change her mind.

In the end we went over to talk to the owner of the funeral home, Mrs Galang. She explained to me that Evelyn, as the wife, took all the decisions – but that she would not do anything with Steven's body until she had been paid. A chink of light opened up for me: everything has a price.

'Please, Evelyn, this means a lot to me. I would like to have my son cremated. We could have it done here. Will you think about it?'

'Yes Ma'am,' she mumbled.

Before I left, I gave her a little money. Later that night I called her and made an offer. I would pay for the funeral if she let me have Steven's ashes. She agreed.

3
Suspicions

In the early hours of Sunday morning, ten days after Steven's death, there was a knock at the door. Unthinkingly, Alan stumbled out of bed to answer the door. There stood three Filipino men. He slammed it shut again.

'God, Marg, there's three guys there.'

'It's the middle of the night! Who are they? What do they want? Call hotel security.' This is it, I thought, we're next.

'Who are you?' Alan called through the door.

'Sorry to disturb, Sir, Ma'am – we are the police from Makati, Manila.'

We looked at each other. What would the police be doing arriving at this time of night? I was sitting there in my nightie, scared half to death.

'Can we see your ID?' Alan asked, opening the door a little.

'No ID, sorry.'

Alan shut the door again. 'They've just got a notebook. Should we trust them? We need to talk to the police, perhaps they're late because it took them ages to get here from Makati, I don't know.' Alan was shaking. What were we getting into?

'Oh, go on. What have we got to lose? Let's take them at face value and find out if there is an investigation. I want to tell them my suspicions. If they're not the police, if they're going to bump us off, at least let it be for a reason.' I was wide awake now and ready for a confrontation.

We let them in.

They sat down politely, and introduced themselves. They were at least wearing uniform, but I shuddered when I noticed they had guns in their holsters.

'We are sorry for your loss, Madam and Sir. We just come to ask you some questions.'

So we told them as much as we knew, and I also made them aware of my suspicions:

1. Evelyn had been taking money from Steven
2. His cashpoint card did not work the day before he died
3. The gunmen used a key to get into his house – how did they get it?
4. Martin could not contact Evelyn for several hours the morning after Steven's death
5. She had not telephoned me at all in the aftermath of his death, and was difficult to get in touch with now
5. She had said that the gunmen were in the house for twenty minutes, but the police said they hadn't told her this.

Each one of these facts might have been fairly flimsy by itself, but taken altogether they sounded like pretty conclusive evidence to me. The men didn't seem convinced, though. Alan kept quiet; he'd decided for the moment to sit on the fence and see what transpired.

'Will you question her?' I asked. They assured me they would, and left us to what remained of the night. Whether they were bona fide police or not, they had gone, and we needed our rest. The funeral was the next day.

The funeral was a very simple Catholic service, held in one of the rooms at the funeral home. It had been arranged by the staff at Steve's office, not by Evelyn, and the place was packed. The coffin was standing in front of the table that served as an altar, and we listened as piped Muzak filled the small space.

I was bursting with emotion, knowing that this was goodbye, my mind crammed with unanswered questions about Steven's death. For the sake of good form, and for the children – little Jessie and even littler Josh, sitting with us in the front pew, next to their mother – I tried not to lose control, forcing myself not to think about what was happening. I tried so hard to block it out I went numb. My palms were sweaty and my throat was dry. Evelyn was pale and still, but betrayed no emotion. I put my arm around her shoulder in an attempt to comfort her, and felt her stiffen. After the sermon the priest motioned us forward to take Communion and I found myself pushing Evelyn towards him – to force her to confront her God. She accepted the bread and wine with a serene expression. As for me, I was angry with God for allowing this to happen; I couldn't imagine ever wanting to take the sacrament again.

When the service had finished the congregation sat silently, waiting for me to move, waiting for something to happen. So I gave Evelyn a warm hug and asked quietly, 'What now, Ev?' She ignored the question, so I asked again, this time in a louder voice. 'You said you would agree to have Steven cremated – what is your decision? What is to happen now? I need to know. I have tried to call you so many times – we need to talk about this.'

'I cannot decide, you are pushing me too much. I leave him here for now. Maybe later I have him buried.'

What? She had promised me. I felt my anger rise, and I started to say something. Alan stepped in. 'Come on, Marg, let's go. We can talk about this tomorrow.' He grabbed me and almost dragged me out. I didn't understand – this was a funeral, and funerals always end with a cremation or a burial, don't they? We couldn't just leave Steven there in this mad country without a resting place. I was having trouble breathing: my head felt as if it would burst.

39

Outside, Brian tried to explain Evelyn's behaviour in the context of his knowledge of Filipina girls. 'She's playing games with you. She has what you want, and she is using Steven as a bargaining chip. She won't bury him, she knows how much his ashes are worth to you.' I couldn't believe that Steve's wife would do this, and I felt he was being unnecessarily cynical.

'Someone is advising her,' Brian insisted. 'I have no idea who, but my feeling is she would not be acting like this on her own.' Unable to control myself, I rushed back into the funeral parlour and confronted her openly.

'Why are you doing this, Evelyn?' I cried. 'You agreed to give me my son – why are you now changing your mind? What do you want from me?'

No one spoke. Then the priest turned towards the assembled company and asked that we all leave in peace. I looked up at him through my tears, and managed to find words to thank him for the service. He took my hand with a sympathetic smile, and said how sorry he was. Alan put his arm around me and we left.

We returned to the hotel feeling drained and confused. I wanted to grieve for my son and I had believed that I would leave the funeral home that day with his ashes. I was exhausted and sad, but my overriding emotion was anger.

'We need to get you away from here,' said Alan that evening. 'Let's leave Evelyn to stew for a few days and go and relax somewhere.'

'I can't, love, I haven't seen the children properly and I can't just leave Steven.'

'We've been here a week and a half. There's not much more we can do for Steven until she decides whether to let you have the cremation. If it's true that she'll do it for money then we can discuss that with her from anywhere, and come back if necessary. She's been keeping the children from you, I know, but I don't see what we can do about that short of busting into her house. And who knows who might be there with her?'

I thought about this, and realised he was right. 'OK, but we're not just going to lie on some beach twiddling our thumbs. We're going to Makati – I want to find out what the police are doing.'

Alan looked at me and nodded wearily. He knew when my mind was made up.

And so it was that the next day we checked out of the hotel and made the three-hour journey back to Makati, the city where Steven was killed and where – so I believed – the investigation into his murder was taking place.

4
The Plot Thickens

It felt good to put some distance between ourselves and Evelyn. The past week and a half had left me feeling angry and bewildered – I had so many questions in my mind about what had really happened that night, and I could not understand why Evelyn was taking such a hard line over Steven's body, but it made me uncomfortable. She was usually so pleasant and compliant. I needed to clear my mind and think about what to do next. But leaving Angeles was also a wrench: I knew my grandchildren needed love and comfort, and I felt Steven would want me to be with them. And no matter how far I travelled from him, the image of Steven lying in cold storage on McArthur Highway remained uppermost in my mind wherever we went and whatever I did. Yet I knew that, for now, I had to keep my grief at bay.

We checked into a low-budget but comfortable hotel – we had stayed there from time to time with Steven and it was conveniently close to his offices. Over breakfast the next morning Alan and I discussed what to do next.

'What's the plan then, Margaret?'

'I don't know. I'm just so worried about the kids. Evelyn is being weird.'

'She's just lost her husband, give her a chance. She probably thinks you're being weird. No one is themselves right now.'

'I know, but we need a strategy to sort this mess out.'

'OK, first things first – what do people usually do? Shouldn't we go to the police station?'

'Yes, we could try to find those guys we saw the other night in Angeles. I wrote down their names. That would be a start.' I tried to collect my thoughts: it was important to be practical rather than emotional. 'I've also got the names of lawyers the Foreign Office man gave me before we left home, and the number of someone in the embassy here. We can decide what to ask them depending on what the police say.'

'Is there any word from your lawyer chap in the UK?'

'No, he sent me an email saying he'd see what he could do. I expect he's working on it – I'll chase him up later.'

So many times over the next few months I would be thankful for my Sony Notebook and my mobile phone. Ironically, if it hadn't been for Steven, I'd still have been in the dark ages technologically – like many of my generation. Just after he had first moved to Hong Kong we had a knock on our front door at home. It was someone carrying large boxes of computer equipment. 'Steven sent me,' he said. 'He wants you to be connected to the internet.' Within a couple of hours we had a state-of-the-art PC in our front room, complete with printer, speakers and modem. We were amazed and delighted – this was Steven all over. I knew why he'd done it – the previous New Year I had been frantic with worry because we had heard about a party in Hong Kong where lots of young people had been hurt. I had called everyone I could think of in an attempt to contact him, terrified that something had happened. He had said then that the internet was the best way to keep in contact when you were in different time zones. So the engineer taught us how to use it, and how to send and receive emails. This became our way of communicating with Steven, and I'd spend hours in 'real time' chats with him using the MSN messenger service. It was a wonderful way of seeing photographs of the children's early years too – Steven even sent us video clips of them down the line. My Notebook – which Steven had also bought for me – had a keypad and a screen, just like a mini-computer, and by attaching a lead from the back of it into a special socket in my hotel room, I could send emails and log on to the internet. Steve called it my 'silver slab'. It would prove to be vital in helping me order my thoughts, make plans, keep records and follow up leads after his death.

The Makati police headquarters was situated in a busy street not far from our hotel. Stepping inside, we took in the gloom, the lack of air-conditioning and the dirty, stained walls. There was an officer sitting in a kiosk, and we took that to be the reception. We introduced ourselves, showed the officer the names of two of the detectives we had met before, and were told to wait. Some time later, another officer appeared and gave us his name. It was Reynoldo Hernandez – we remembered him from that unexpected visit in Angeles. So they were proper policemen after all. Phew.

'I am homicide-investigating officer,' he said. 'Please follow me.'

We were led through a large room, empty but for several old bench tables and white plastic chairs. At the end of the room were doorless cubicles, each with a sign indicating the purpose to which each was put: 'Incident', 'Follow-Up Squad', 'Homicide', I read. We knew which was ours: it was sparsely furnished with an old table and wooden bench, and a couple of plastic chairs. The floor was filthy, and on the table rested a battered 1930s typewriter and a clapped-out computer. Not exactly confidence-inspiring, I thought to myself.

'What is the news, officer?' I asked, deciding to take the lead.

'We have no new information, Ma'am,' he replied. 'But we are hoping for some to come up soon. The situation is ongoing.'

45

'Have you interviewed my son's wife?' I asked.

'No, that would be unusual. We have a witness, Mr Martin, and he gave us a lot of help.'

Unusual? I looked at Alan.

'Yes, we know you have a photofit picture of the suspect. How are you using it?' I asked.

'Martin was very traumatised the day we did the photofit. I worry that it may not be very accurate. But we are looking into it.'

I realised I was going to have to use my best powers of persuasion if he felt it was unusual to interview a wife. 'When we saw you in Angeles, officer, I explained that I felt there were some very worrying aspects to the murder, and it seemed as if Steven's wife could be very helpful to you in clarifying some of those questions.'

'That is possible, Ma'am, but we have to wait for her to make a complaint.'

'A complaint? What do you mean?'

'I mean that our legal system here in the Philippines requires a person to be the injured party, and for that person to make representations to the police for investigations to take place.'

'What about me? Can I be the injured party? I'm ready to make a complaint.' I sure was.

'I'm sorry to say that it should be the next of kin, which is the wife. I expect she will do it but at the moment she is too upset.' Not from what I saw she wasn't.

'Is it true that when Evelyn identified the body, she was already dressed in mourning clothes?' We had been given this piece of information the night the police came to our hotel room, and I suddenly remembered it now.

'She was wearing black, yes. And when I asked her if she was all right, she . . .' here he hesitated. '. . . She mentioned that Steven had an insurance policy and a house in England.'

My heart started beating faster than normal. Was this evidence of forward planning?

'What did you say to that?'

'Nothing, but my colleague agreed with me that this was a strange thing for a Filipina widow to say.'

'I'm worried about the children,' I then said, having digested this information. 'It is not a good environment for them to be in.'

'They are with their mother: that is normal,' he replied.

'Can I at least take them to England for a holiday?'

'Yes, if you have passports for them and if the mother gives you permission, of course. That is not police business.' I made a note of this.

I returned to the issue of the 'complaint': 'Can I ask, officer, what happens if the wife – for her own reasons – does not want to come to the police station? Can you bring her in for questioning?'

'Only if we have a reason to do so. If we bring somebody in and cannot make a case against them we are not permitted to interview them again, even if new evidence comes up. At the moment there is no evidence against Mrs Davis. This case looks to us like a robbery that went wrong.'

We weren't making any progress, but I realised I would not gain anything by making a fuss right now. We shook hands and bade the officer a polite goodbye, making our exit through the large room. In one corner a group of detectives were sitting around a television screen laughing. They were watching American cartoons.

We walked the few blocks back to the hotel in silence, both stunned by the rank amateurishness of what we had just witnessed, and dismayed that we seemed to have reached an impasse.

'Well – that's it then,' said Alan eventually. 'We've got to persuade Evelyn to make her complaint, and perhaps they'll get going properly.' Dear, naïve Alan – did he really think she was going to do this? It seemed plain as a pikestaff to me that she would be content to move on with her life whether or not the murderer was found. This wasn't good enough for me. My mind was racing with grief and anger, and a need to do something.

'This is how I see it,' I said. 'The police don't seem willing to do anything more than wait and see. Martin gave them a picture, Evelyn knows more than she is letting on, I'm convinced of it. In fact there must be loads of people to question. If they need a reason to interview her, I'll give them a reason.'

'Steady on, love. You haven't got any proof. I know these police guys don't do things the way we'd expect back home, but shouldn't we give them a chance to get their investigation under way?'

'That's as may be,' I harrumphed, kicking our hotel bedroom door open. I had to try to get control of my fury. Despite what Alan said, I was sure the police weren't doing enough, and nor were the lawyers – either here or back home.

That evening we sat in the hotel bar. Alan was hunched over, holding his grief in, brooding over our spat earlier. I was thinking, thinking. Who could help us? I would persevere with the police and planned to visit them daily, but who else was there? I called the Foreign Office in London. They made the right noises, but were clearly unable to do anything practical to help. I needed a lawyer on the ground, and the next morning I dug out the list I had been given the day after Steven died. I dialled number after number: some were out of order; others just rang and rang. Some relayed incomprehensible voicemail messages; others were answered by receptionists who promised but failed to have someone call me back. Just as I was beginning to despair I got through to an attorney who not only answered the phone himself, but also spoke reasonable English and sounded efficient. His name was Christian Aguera and he asked me for $10,000 to take on my case. I swallowed hard, trying to keep my temper, and negotiated him down to a quarter of this amount.

It was just as well that I had made contact with him, because on our next visit to the police station Reynoldo explained that if I was prepared to be the 'complainant' it might move things forward, and if so, could I please draw up an affidavit.

'A what?'

'A statement signed by you and checked by a lawyer, which gives all the information you know about the circumstances leading up to your son's death.'

This could be the breakthrough we had waited for, and I was only too glad to do it – only I had no idea where to start. What would I say? How 'hard' did my facts have to be? How could I fit it into the Filipino legal system? I was thrown into confusion, and my response was to reach for my trusty silver slab. It took me several days to prepare this document, but at least I felt I was doing something.

Every conversation we had had over the past two weeks revolved around what might have happened. Every day several wild theories spun through my mind. Alan was inclined to believe it was a botched robbery – but if so, why were Steven's mobile and watch not stolen? Was there any way it could have been a corporate killing designed to put Steve's company out of business? We felt this was unlikely, as Martin would surely have been killed too – he was a director and was in the house at the time. Had Steven on a personal level been involved in anything that he should not have been? This was difficult to know, and as parents, naturally we trusted that Steve was honourable and decent. His friends and colleagues also assured us that Steven did not have a wild life and had had many friends who respected and admired him. We knew he had done a great deal of charity work. No, there was no evidence that Steven was anything but a good, honest man. So good, in fact, that he had for years doled out money to Evelyn and her family without question – until recently. I felt sure that money was at the root of this. He had talked about cutting off Evelyn's allowance – was her family getting worried that their source of income would disappear? If so, surely it would have been madness to kill him, and cut off the source of all the cash?

As for me, I had been concerned for some time about what was happening to Steve's money. In January of that year we had arrived in Angeles for a three-month stay. The normal pattern would be that Steven would work during the week in Makati, and return to Angeles on Friday night. We would stay in the house with Evelyn and the children. It had struck us that things were not quite right when we had realised that Evelyn was rising early and disappearing for most of the day, leaving Jessica and Joshua with the maid. It is quite usual for expatriates and the wealthier Filipinos to have a live-in maid to cook, clean and help take care of the children. We had been surprised at first, but it's something that is totally accepted in many Asian countries, so we got used to it. It is a system that does after all offer employment to people who would otherwise be on the streets. I must admit, when Jessica was first born I didn't like seeing Evelyn lie in bed all day while the maids took care of all the domestic chores. I told Steve one day that his wife was lazy. 'Evelyn doesn't have to do anything, Mum, she's my princess,' he replied. Don't interfere, I told myself.

Anyway, during our stay Evelyn would come back late at night, and sometimes not at all. One week the water, electricity and telephone were all cut off due to unpaid bills. Getting them reconnected was a simple matter of taking the cash to the various utility companies, but Steven was furious. That weekend – sweltering in a dark house without aircon, unable to wash and with candles as our only source of light – we heard them arguing about it, Evelyn claiming to have paid the bills but unable to find the receipts. I tried to talk to Steven about it a few days later, but he was clearly hurt and embarrassed, and I did not press the matter. 'She's moody and difficult sometimes, Mum, that's all,' he'd said. Dealing with Evelyn that week was like walking on eggshells – I knew that if I was seen to be taking sides I risked ruining our relationship, in which case we would never be welcome in her house again. Alan and I discussed the situation many times, and at length we agreed that there were some things about the country we would never understand, but we accepted the choices Steven had made and we would support him in whatever he did. 'Each to his own, Marg, each to his own,' was Alan's refrain. I agreed, we had no right to make judgements about what we thought was right or wrong. We respected what Steven wanted and respected what he loved. This was his marriage and we had to go along with what went with it.

I remember well that Monday morning when Steven left for work. I got up at 5 am to have breakfast with him before he left, and we enjoyed coffee and toast outside. Early mornings in the tropics are the best times – the air is warm, the light is soft and golden, and the grass and trees give off fragrant scents. Rather like an English summer's day, I always felt – except for the knowledge that it would turn humid and unbearably hot later on. Steven was smart in a crisp white shirt and khaki chinos, and we had a comfortable chat under the gazebo in his garden – he was looking forward to getting stuck into his work that week, and I talked about what I might do with the kids. It is memories such as these that I will always cherish.

That week, however, things went from bad to worse. Someone turned up to collect the rent and had a noisy argument with Evelyn on their doorstep, during which she seemed to be claiming that it had been paid. 'Where is the receipt?' I asked. 'I don't know, Ma'am. I have lost it,' she replied, not catching my eye. Alan shot me a warning look, and out of earshot said, 'This is Steven's business, Marg. Don't get involved, don't say anything stupid.'

My goodness, there were tears that weekend – Evelyn finally admitted that she had not paid the rent, but protested that she had given the money to a sick aunt who could claim the money back from her health insurance after an operation. I laughed when I heard this – no one in Evelyn's village could afford medical insurance. What on earth was at the bottom of all this? Steven was at his wits' end: 'You must stop your family pressurising you for money, Ev, they've had enough. And I've had enough.' She seemed to agree, and for a few days she tried hard to please everyone, eating with us and chatting in a friendly fashion. Steven seemed to put it behind him; I couldn't, but perhaps I had an over-developed maternal instinct.

That was just a few months ago.

'Could it really be possible that Evelyn – or her family – would bring about Steven's death in order to benefit from his life insurance?' I said to Alan.

'I suppose it's possible, anything's possible – but they are simple folk. And they relied on Steven. Do you remember how they used to leave the house with whatever they could carry – lightbulbs, rice-cookers, water-filters, pillows and all sorts – to take back to their villages? Steven used to laugh and say it was the least he could do for them. He had a very strong sense of responsibility, and I think he felt guilty for being so wealthy simply because of where he had been born.'

'I call that thieving, not simple-minded borrowing or

whatever,' I retorted. 'Steven was way too good to them. He paid Ev the equivalent of £1,000 a month for household bills, but somehow the bills weren't paid and all that money disappeared. These people live cheaply! How could they be spending this amount?'

'There's no national health service here, Margaret. Medical bills are astronomical, and there was the sick aunt.'

'Oh, leave it out,' I said, exasperated. 'One sick aunt and all that loot? It doesn't stack up.'

'Maybe not,' replied Alan. 'But to kill the golden goose? Never.'

I didn't want to argue with Alan over this. Instead I called the bank in Hong Kong and asked for a printout of the ATM withdrawals the week before Steven died – perhaps that would throw something up.

Alan always stuck up for the underdog, and I admired this quality in him. But for me, things were beginning to add up. Was Steven being made a fool of? Or did he realise what was going on and was turning a blind eye because of his charitable instincts? Either way, something underhand had been going on.

That afternoon I telephoned the British Consulate to see if they could help, and we were invited in to meet one of the diplomats, Peter Hawkins. He had a large, plush office – and on a board by his desk were pinned several notices concerning incidents involving Brits in the Philippines: 'Man mugged in Manila . . . Girl in hospital with serious injuries . . . Murder in Makati – Steven Davis.'

My blood froze. We were here because of Steven, of course, but I hadn't expected it to be so public.

Questions rushed out of me – why had the body been embalmed so quickly? Why hadn't the wife been interviewed? How could I repatriate the body to the UK? What should I do about the children? My son's wife had been taking large amounts of money out of their household account, why wasn't she being questioned? Mr Hawkins calmly poured me a cup of tea.

'Mrs Davis, I agree this is a tricky situation, and I gather the police have started their investigation. I'm sure they will be exploring every avenue.' His voice was educated and smooth.

'That's as may be, but we saw the officer in charge of the investigation this morning, and we are concerned that the police do not seem to be following any sort of formal procedure. They are not following up basic leads that would be the obvious first thing for British police to look into.'

'Things happen very differently here,' said Mr Hawkins in soothing tones, 'and if they seem to be doing things slowly it does not necessarily mean they are not doing it correctly. I'm sure you'll appreciate that we cannot interfere with the work of the police.'

This was a nightmare; we weren't going to get anywhere with this, so I tried a different tack: 'What about the children?'

'If you can get their mother to sign passport forms we will see about getting them visas.' OK, that would have to be a priority. 'But to be frank, my concern is for your own safety.'

'What do you mean?'

'First, we cannot be sure why your son was killed, and the murderer may have reason to target you too. Secondly, Filipino people are clannish and very protective of their own – if they feel that one of their own has been insulted or offended, they may want to come after you in some way. There is an "eye for an eye" mentality that you should be aware of.' He then suggested we move to a safer, more expensive hotel in a smarter area of the city. I was advised not to wear any visible jewellery or use a mobile phone in public.

We asked about Steven's body, and what the correct protocol would be. Peter agreed with our feelings that it was distinctly odd that there had been on forensic tests, on post-mortem, and that the move to embalm him was very quick. But all he could do was encourage us to speak to Evelyn, and negotiate a payment. Was he giving us *carte blanche* to offer her a bribe?

'I assure you I will take a great personal interest in this case.' His concern seemed genuine, and I trusted that he would do all he could to help us. On our way out he handed me passport forms for the children.

Once back at the hotel, I collapsed onto the bed and sobbed. This was hard, so hard, and I did not know how long it was to go on for. The prospect of days in this dirty, chaotic city – talking to officials, trying my best to be efficient, organised and logical – filled me with dread. My thoughts turned to the fatherless children back in Angeles. Was Jessie weeping for her daddy? They'd been so close, Steven had adored her – it would be a very strange time for the little girl. As for Josh, he was only a baby, but he'd enjoyed the rough-and-tumble times and Steve was fiercely proud to have a son. He always did a lot for the kids – changing nappies, organising vaccinations, buying food, taking them for days out. I remember the pride in his voice when he told me how he took Jessica up in a microlight plane at Angeles City Flying Club: 'Jess is so brave, Mum – she was so excited up in the air!' Somehow Evelyn had never struck me as particularly maternal, but Steve had always told me this was a cultural thing. Filipina girls are simply not as emotional about children as we are, he had explained, partly because in many rural parts of the country they are still expected to grow up quickly and earn a living.

I turned over in my mind that conversation at the funeral parlour when Evelyn had told me she was pregnant again. And a horrible suspicion entered my mind. She hadn't told Steven she was pregnant – why? Could it have been because the baby *was not his*? I knew relations weren't that good between them, and she had the children in bed with her most nights. Was it possible she had a lover? And did she delay telling Steven about her pregnancy because it was not yet showing? And was she – dear God – was she fearing what his reaction might be when it did become clear that she was pregnant?

It was true about Filipina girls not being emotional about children. Evelyn had been pregnant the previous time we had visited them, which perhaps explained her extreme moodiness. The moment we arrived I realised she had put on weight, and I guessed she must have been four or five months pregnant. Why hadn't Steven mentioned it to me? I asked her outright one morning, and she admitted that, yes, she was indeed pregnant.

'But I not feel good with this baby. Like Joshua I feel sick all the time.'

'Another boy then, that's wonderful news!' I replied, feeling the need to jolly her along. Male babies were always a cause for joy in the Philippines. I wondered if she would let me name this new baby, as I had been allowed to do with Joshua. I liked the name Daniel. Jessie, Joshua and Daniel: it had a nice ring to it. But Evelyn just shook her head, looking miserable.

'What about Steve, does he know?' I asked, fishing for more information. She shrugged her shoulders then and retreated into her bedroom, clearly not wanting to discuss it. Don't get involved, Margaret, I told myself, for the umpteenth time. It was quite possible Steven didn't know – he was away during the week and, like many men, might not pick up the signs the way women tend to. I hoped that when he returned in a few days she would tell him; I hated to think there might be something I knew that he didn't.

I will never know if she did confess or not, because a week later something awful happened. As I sat in my hotel room after we'd had that first meeting at the British Consulate, it all came back to me with terrible clarity. One day Evelyn had disappeared from the house in the early morning, leaving the children at home with one of the maids. She did not return until the following morning, and I was waiting for her. It was time to ask some more questions.

'What's up, Evelyn?' I asked.

'Nothing, Ma'am,' she replied, refusing to catch my eye. 'All everything fine.'

'Evelyn love, we've been worried sick about you. The children have been asking after you. Where were you last night? Is something wrong? Look at me, come on. I might be able to help.'

She sank onto the sofa and put her head in her hands.

'OK, Ma'am, I tell you my trouble. I no want this baby.' She looked up at me, eyes desperate. 'It is wrong time. I want to study, I want learn to drive, many things. I no want this baby.'

I sighed. I had always been trying to persuade her to learn to read, to better herself – but what a way to tell me she wanted to do more with her life.

'Evelyn, listen. This is something for you to discuss with Steven.' I could sense I was getting into deep water. There must be another reason for her not wanting this baby – she could still learn to read and drive after it was born.

'Ma'am, I no want this baby,' she repeated. 'I worry for five months already. This baby no good, I take medicine to get baby out.' I reeled. What? Was this where she had been all day? I wasn't sure whether to believe her.

The next morning she left before we woke up, leaving no word as to where she was going or when she would be back. There was no food in the house, so Alan and I took the children out to eat, and we had a nice afternoon in the botanical gardens, pushing Josh in his buggy and pointing out the huge red blooms of the flame trees to Jessie. The vegetation in that part of the world never failed to amaze me with its lushness, its over-ripeness. It was a humid day, and we were hot and in need of a shower when we returned. Still no sign of Evelyn, and the children were fed and fast asleep in bed by the time she returned.

It was about half past nine. She went straight into the shower, and I found her ten minutes later in the kitchen wearing just a tee-shirt. There was blood on the white tiles of the floor. I stared at it. 'You're bleeding, Evelyn.'

'I know. It is the baby. It does not want to stay inside my body.' She cried out then, doubling up in pain.

'Come to the bathroom, my love.' I guided her into the shower, and there she stood in her nightgown as a bloody mass slithered out from between her legs. The baby. It was on the floor of the shower, next to our feet. A five-month-old foetus.

'We must get you to hospital, come on,' I eventually managed to blurt out. I could see that she was bleeding very heavily.

'No, I will be fine. No hospital. This is what we do in the provinces if we don't want baby. Please, Ma'am, go away.'

So I went. Alan was sitting outside under a lovely gazebo we had bought for the house, around which Steven had strung up fairy lights. We had thought it was beautiful, but suddenly it looked tawdry and pointless, like Christmas decorations in January. I'm sure I must have told Alan what had happened, but I don't remember saying anything, just sitting there.

And then suddenly there was Evelyn, carrying the baby in a plastic bag in one hand and a carving knife in the other. She showed it to us, and Alan asked if it was one of the children's hamsters that the dog had attacked.

'No, it's my baby,' she said simply. Alan looked aghast. All I could think was, 'Daniel. That is Daniel.'

Evelyn knelt down and hacked a lump of turf off the lawn with the knife, plonked the plastic bag and its contents on to the earth, and put the piece of grass back on top. Then she trod on it. Was this her idea of a burial? At least say a prayer, I thought. At least give him a name. I reached out for Alan and we sat there, silently, for a long time. We were both weeping. There are some visions that stay in your mind all your life, and for the rest of my days I will remember two things: one is Steven lying dead in his coffin, and the other is that poor little baby in its plastic bag.

At last I got up and went to Evelyn. She was still bleeding but refused to let me help her, so I just advised her to go to bed and raise her legs to slow the bleeding.

I couldn't sleep that night, wondering if I should phone Steven, worrying about Evelyn, mourning the child who never was. I got up about half past five and went to check on Evelyn. She was asleep, but I had never seen her such a strange colour – not her usual lovely brown, but a pallid yellow. I pulled the sheets back, and there was blood everywhere, spreading out from where she lay to the edge of the bed. Calling to one of the maids to get Evelyn ready, I phoned Steven and told him his wife had miscarried in the night and was bleeding profusely.

'Take her to hospital, Mum,' he begged. 'I don't want to be responsible for my wife bleeding to death. Look after her, please don't let anything happen to her.' Then he said, almost to himself, it seemed, 'I had no idea she was pregnant. I've hardly been home the last few months – I wonder when she conceived?'

We carried her into a taxi, and to a hospital – where the doctor gave her a good telling-off. She had seen plenty of cases like this before, I guessed. I felt sorry for Evelyn: she was so sick, and here she was being given a right bollocking. Then the doctor turned to me. 'She's going to need an operation right now to stop the bleeding. The placenta has not fully detached and she is haemorrhaging. Without this operation she will die.'

'Save her,' I said without hesitation.

'You must pay first. Twelve thousand peso.' So I paid, and I saved Evelyn's life.

Now, sitting in this expensive hotel room several months later, I felt the realisation dawn on me like a sickness. I knew exactly why Steven had been killed. It had to be Evelyn – she had been having an affair. She was pregnant with her lover's baby and was terrified Steven really would throw her out when the pregnancy started to show. He had already threatened to cut off her allowance if the loans to her family did not stop.

'Alan,' I called. He was in the bathroom shaving. 'Alan, come here, I need to talk to you.'

He came out, towel at his face. 'What is it? What's up? You look as if you've seen a ghost.'

'I've got it, love. I think I know what happened.' Shaking, I told him my suspicions. And for once Alan didn't try to dissuade me.

'So you think the men who did it,' he said slowly, 'were hired by Evelyn to do her dirty work.'

'And paid with Steven's money,' I said bitterly. Poor, foolish Steven. Cheated on by a cruel and greedy wife, and then murdered.

'Steven may have been the golden goose, like you say, but remember that in the story the golden goose gets killed.'

'Be sure, Margaret. You must be sure. She's greedy and materialistic, but a murderer?' As ever, the voice of reason.

I had never felt surer in my life – all my mother's instincts told me I was right. It all fitted. My job now was to prove to the police that I was right, and I was determined to do this for Steven if it was the last thing I did.

Alan and I clung to each other that night, overflowing with grief for our dear son.

5
I Take Matters Into My Own Hands

The next morning I awoke feeling renewed vigour. Steven had not been dead two weeks and already I felt I had a complete understanding of what had happened to him. Despite Alan's warnings, in the absence of any other information I was going to proceed on this basis. I had already made a few notes on the silver slab, and I now started to turn them into more of a diary. I went out and bought a pad of A3 paper, marker pens and some drawing pins. I also found several books on Philippine law and culture. They had titles like *Understanding Filipino Values on Love, Sex and Marriage*, *The Family Code of the Philippines* and *Negotiating by Filipino Values*. I was hoping they would help me understand what I was up against. My final purchase was a tape recorder and a microphone. Our hotel room would become the centre of operations for the next few weeks, and I was determined to stay on top of events and arm myself with everything I needed.

Alan watched as I made lists of things to do and pinned them up around the room. One poster read:

EVELYN – SUSPICIOUS THINGS
– wore black to identify body
– very keen to find out what Martin saw
– is pregnant, already had one secret abortion
– was taking money from Steven
– was arguing with Steven

WE NEED TO KNOW
– whose baby is it?
– where was she at the time of the murder?
– why was she unobtainable the next morning?
– bank account information?
– where was the money going?
– who were the people who used to come to Steve's house when he was away?
– who were the 3 gunmen?

STEVEN – QUESTIONS
– was he in trouble business-wise?
– what happened to his door key?
– why couldn't he use his ATM card?
– who tried to use his ATM card the day after he died? (the bank statement had revealed that someone had tried and failed to withdraw money)
– had something happened between him and Evelyn recently?

OTHER THINGS TO DO
– help the children in some way (very important)
– get Steven cremated
– try to get his ashes afterwards
– talk to the police

I completed my affidavit later that day and showed it to Alan. He looked impressed.

'I didn't know you had this in you, Margaret. You're becoming a bit of an expert in this stuff.'

'Yeah, well, it's amazing what you can do when you have to. Let's go and get it signed and sealed, then it's over to the police.' Our lawyer read it briefly and signed it no problem, but the process of authorising it at the police station was surreal. First I had to take it to a photocopy shop because the police station copier was broken. Then we were led down a narrow dirty alleyway to another building, through a maze of stairs and corridors to a tiny room piled high with files. Hidden behind the files was a man eating his lunch. Reynoldo Hernandez thrust our file at him and he put down his rice bowl to read it. No one spoke for a long time. Then the man stood up, and motioned me to stand too.

'What is your name?' he asked solemnly.

'Margaret Davis.'

He gave me a copy of the Bible. 'Do you swear this is the absolute truth?'

I put my hand on the Bible and said, 'I swear.'

And that was it. We walked back to the main building, and I asked for a further talk with Reynoldo. I wanted to explain, very carefully and as clearly as I could, who I thought had masterminded the murder, and what the possible motives might have been. He had my affidavit, and I wanted him to be aware of its contents. So far he had not read it and, as he was in charge of the investigation, I decided to help him along. I knew I had to control my voice, which was shaking with emotion, and not betray the rising anger I was feeling about what I saw as Evelyn's involvement. If the police felt I was driven by a personal vendetta, jealousy or a mean-spirited desire to see Steven's wife in trouble, I would not be taken seriously.

Reynoldo took in what I was saying, making notes and nodding. I finished speaking, and he looked at me.

'Here are some photos you should see.' He opened a file and handed me a plastic wallet. Inside were several photos of my son, dead. One showed how his arm had been pierced by two bullets – these would not have killed him. The other showed two dark bullet holes underneath one arm – they had pierced his heart and lungs. This meant he would have had time to wake up, feel mortal fear, put his hands up, beg for mercy. I felt sick and turned away, suddenly forgetting that I was at the police station. Instead, I was in the room with Steven as the gunmen burst in, I felt him raising his arm in self-defence, I heard him pleading with them not to shoot. Then everything went blurred.

Alan spoke for me.

'Please, Sir, can you interview Evelyn now, or at least go to Angeles City to investigate the situation?'

There was an uncomfortable pause. 'We would like to help,' Reynoldo replied eventually, 'but regretfully we have no budget for this.'

I swallowed hard, and pulled myself together. 'What do you mean, budget? Surely it is normal practice to investigate a murder by following up all the leads?' Alan gave me a warning nudge – he knew I was perilously close to offending them. 'I mean, I know you have been working so hard already, it would be a shame to leave it now.'

'These investigations are expensive. We need money for petrol, food, stationery and other expenses.' Oh, right. The penny dropped. I reached into my bag and drew out 10,000 pesos (about £120).

'Will this be enough to get you started?' It jolly well should be, I thought. This guy's weekly salary was less than a quarter of that.

'Yes, Ma'am, thank you. I will send four officers to Angeles today, and I will let you know the results of their investigations.' This was the way to get things done in the Philippines. I didn't see the money as a bribe – budgets were tight, I knew that. But it did make me angry to think that not everyone would be able to afford to assist an investigation.

'Thank you. I would like to photocopy the information you already have in your file, please. And could you also telephone Mrs Galang at the funeral parlour to ask her to release my son's body for cremation?' I handed him the number.

'Of course.'

Hallelujah. This was no small triumph, and we felt a little encouraged as we left the station and walked downtown towards the City Hall.

'Well done, Marg,' said Alan. 'You're financing the investigation – they'll have to tell you everything now.'

'Yes, well, fine for us who can pay. Don't they call it chequebook justice? I wonder how many other murders of poor local people go ignored and unsolved?' I was feeling weak at the thought of those bullet holes in Steven's side. I still had the photo in my bag.

A little later that day there would be another thing in my bag that I would rather not have had to see. Steven's death certificate, which we were collecting from the City Hall on the advice of Peter Hawkins at the Foreign Office. Under normal circumstances it would be collected by the wife. Yet again, Evelyn had let Steven down. The death certificate was only half filled in, and under 'Cause of death' it said 'gunshot wounds.' What on earth were they doing, then, allowing his body to be embalmed so quickly? And, strangely, under 'Address of Next of Kin' Evelyn had put an address I did not recognise. Needless to say, the police were not interested in this anomaly.

Although we were staying in Makati I kept calling Evelyn to see if I could come and see the children in Angeles. I was ready to make the three-hour journey in a moment once she gave the word. I kept thinking of the little ones, and how sad Jessie would be. She would be starting to miss her daddy terribly now – and might even be asking for me and Alan. Yet every time I called Evelyn was out, and all I could do was leave messages. Who was looking after the children, I wondered. I also surmised that by now Evelyn would be pretty desperate for money, so perhaps a mention of cash would induce her to call me back.

We made daily visits to the police station, waiting and hoping for information. It was awful, the powerlessness of waiting, when every day seemed like a week. Each day we asked hopefully if there was news, and each day they said they had no leads. They got to know us well, and were always ready with chairs and polite smiles. If I was becoming an irritation to them, they did not make it obvious. We learnt that they had 'invited' Evelyn to come to the station in Makati three times, and each time she had refused. Three times? This was getting ridiculous – surely they could force her to come in? One day I had to buy carbon paper before a report on the first few days' investigations could be typed up. Carbon paper! I hadn't seen that for about fifteen years. These guys were working in the Dark Ages. It was easy to feel disheartened, and one morning as we were gloomily waiting to see Reynoldo an officer approached me.

'Ma'am, I am sorry for your distress.' I looked up questioningly. This wasn't one of the police officers we usually dealt with.

'I can get this done for a price, Madam. And I can also get your son's body for you.' I was stunned. What was he suggesting? I looked at Alan for guidance. Seeing my confusion, the officer went on: 'Anything is possible, for money, here in the Philippines.'

Oh my God! He was suggesting a vigilante killing – an eye for an eye. My blood froze and my heart thumped in my chest. Could I do this? Should I? I had a moment's indecision, then sense flooded back.

'Maybe. Thank you.' I had a desperate need to get out of the building. Not just budgetary constraints and a lack of purpose, amongst the police. Murder too, for a price. I was beginning to despise this country – every day we'd see reports

68

of murders, rapes and armed robberies. It seemed as if we were drowning in a hellish sea of crime, and what was worse was that these events were happening on our doorstep: a restaurant we liked was attacked by gunmen; missionaries on an island we had once visited were beheaded by terrorists. I despaired of ever finding justice for Steven in a country that seemed to value life so little. The tears I shed every night for my dear Steven were mingled with hot rage at his loss and frustration at the slowness of solving the murder. What more should I be doing?

A few days after this we received a call from Peter Hawkins at the British Embassy in Manila. The staff at the embassy were the representatives of Her Majesty's government in the Philippines, and if anyone could help us, they could.

'The ambassador would like to see you to discuss your case. He will send a car for you at 11 am.' Wow, we thought, could this be progress at last? We dressed carefully, and collected our thoughts for the important meeting ahead. I must say we couldn't help feeling rather grand as the sleek car whisked us through Manila – traffic lights and check-points no problem with diplomatic number plates – to an imposing mansion in a secure area of the city.

We were ushered into a study where we met the ambassador and his wife. A uniformed maid poured coffee from a silver pot and handed round tiny little chocolate biscuits.

'What a dreadful situation you are in,' said the ambassador. 'We have been kept up to date by Peter Hawkins with the current progress.'

'Or lack of,' I interrupted, knowing I was being rude. 'Can you tell us why the police aren't being very active?' He couldn't. In fact, all he could do was tell me what he couldn't do. He couldn't interfere, he couldn't advise, he couldn't question, he couldn't draft in extra help.

That wasn't good enough for me. 'I need to know what you *can* do,' I insisted. 'Look at us. We are an ordinary British couple caught up in a nightmare situation. Our son has been murdered, and we suspect his wife. There is plenty of circumstantial evidence. You have to help us. Please.'

'I have spoken with the officers in Makati and I believe they are doing all they can. I'm afraid you must try to accept what they are doing, and not offend them by questioning their methods, their intelligence, or their lack of resources.'

'They may well be perfectly intelligent, but surely there is a protocol to follow when someone is murdered? Is life so cheap that death is not investigated?'

'Things are done differently here. As ambassador, I'm afraid I cannot get involved in local politics.'

Typical Foreign Office, I thought. I was getting angry, and deliberately ignored Alan's warning glances. 'What is your role here, then, if not to take an interest in a British subject who is murdered? Surely you could have let the relatives know. Surely you could ensure that a proper investigation is being carried out. There were no forensic tests, the evidence was destroyed, and the body was embalmed almost immediately. The police know who they want to interview, but they are passively waiting for her to offer herself up. How can they solve any murders if this is the way they carry on? It seems to me that this is a case of "Here's a Western guy who's been murdered, let's hush it up quickly."'

The ambassador was shifting uneasily in his seat. I almost felt sorry for him, but I had things to say and I was going to say them. Our conversation continued unsatisfactorily for a few minutes, until he looked at his watch.

'You do have my sympathy, I assure you. I'm afraid I now have a lunch party to attend – you are both more than welcome to stay and meet other expats who live in these islands. There will be lots of other British and American people, you might enjoy it.'

I looked at him in astonishment. 'I don't think we are in the mood for a party,' was the politest response I could manage.

'What a farce,' commented Alan as the car sped us back to our hotel. 'His intentions are good, but he can't do a thing to help. He was just warning us off.'

'Well, he's not going to warn *me* off,' I muttered grimly. I wasn't surprised at the lack of official help: I had come to expect it. We were in this alone.

Whiling away the hours in our hotel room, waiting for news – from the police, from Evelyn, from my lawyer back home – I felt I was slowly going out of my mind. My nails were bitten to the quick, I was losing weight, my skin and hair looked awful. To distract myself from the wait I absorbed myself in the books I had bought. They made interesting reading. I learnt about the culture of revenge killing in the Philippines, and how easy it is to have someone bumped off for a little money. I read about the people who live in the provinces: some never leave the villages they are born in, and grow up believing ancient superstitions involving strange legends, witchcraft and demons, and never learn to read and write. They believe that foreigners are evil, and when things go wrong families gang together against those they see as the enemy. I asked Reynoldo's boss Ramon Tampinco about this. 'It can be true, yes. The village people are different from the city people.' I told him where Evelyn's family was from and he looked alarmed. 'Ah, yes. These people can be dangerous; your son should have learnt more about them. A Western man marrying a Filipina is marrying her entire family, and he may find the sweet kitten becomes an angry tiger if things do not go her way. You two must also be careful.'

That night, lying awake, exhausted but unable to sleep, the events and conversations of the day spinning around my mind, I had an idea. I needed someone with local knowledge who understood this village mentality. Someone who moved in the right circles and who wouldn't be scared to dig around a little. If the police couldn't ask their own questions, I decided, I would find someone to go and ask some questions for me. This surely counted as 'being careful'. I called Brian at Steven's office and asked his advice.

'You should talk to Paco, he worked with Steve for years. He's a local lad, knows all sorts of people.' Of course, I'd met him four years ago in Hong Kong, and I knew he worked in the Makati office. Steven had been a kind of mentor to him, and had helped him in his career. I called him and explained we were having trouble finding out what had really happened to Steve. Straight off he told me something that brought my heart into my mouth.

'I have a friend, Miguel Garcia, who works here. He said Evelyn had a boyfriend.'

At last – our suspicions confirmed.

'Who is it? Do you know the name?'

'Sorry, I don't know. He had a motorbike, Miguel said, and one day I also saw her talking to a man on a bike. She was holding baby Joshua.'

We talked a little more about the police investigation, and he sounded obviously upset about the loss of his friend and employer. He gave me Miguel's number, and asked if there was anything else he could do.

'Paco, I have to find out what happened to my son, and I want to help the police with their investigation. I am looking for someone who could do a little detective work for me. Is there anyone you can think of who might be able to do this?' He said he would think about it and call me back later. I thanked him and said goodbye, wondering what I had started. Perhaps it would be better if he didn't know anyone after all, and half of me hoped he wouldn't call back. I didn't tell Alan about my plan.

Nevertheless, in a state of some excitement I called the police with this new information about Evelyn's apparent boyfriend, and gave them the number to call. Very politely, Reynoldo told me there was not much he could do. Remembering I needed to keep them on side, I swallowed my disgust, but I could not speak to him any longer.

'How can they not see what we can see?' I raged to Alan after slamming the phone down. 'It's so obvious! Why can't they just interview the boyfriend? What are they so afraid of?'

'I think they're just waiting for us to get fed up and go home.'

'Not until my son's killer is behind bars.'

Later that afternoon Paco phoned me back. He said he knew someone who worked as a security guard in Angeles. I agreed to meet them both at the hotel the following day.

It was time to tell Alan what I was planning. He hit the roof.

'What? You can't be serious – I know these security types, they carry guns, they know all sorts of disreputable people, they'll do anything for money. You must be mad, Margaret – here we are, in the middle of a murder investigation, and you're inviting strangers to your room. This is the Philippines – there are bad, shady people, they inhabit the underworld. Surely we should stick with the police.'

'I don't know what else to do. I know it's a risk, but frankly I don't feel we've got much to lose.' My voice had a hysterical edge, and I could hear it. 'From what I've seen, the police are just as bad, any road.'

'Nothing to lose? What about our own lives? I don't expect you're exactly flavour of the month with Evelyn

73

and her family right now – you've blocked her bank account and no doubt she's bricking herself now that the police have asked her three times to go in for questioning. How do you know that these two guys aren't in league with her? Steven was killed in an instant.' He snapped his fingers. 'Who's to say we won't be? You're the main beneficiary of Steven's will. You're in the way.'

'You don't understand! My son is dead, I have to do this. Steven would want me to.'

It wasn't exactly an argument, but we were both by this stage worn out by worry, fear and frustration. I knew that Alan had to back me up in this, and it took a long time to convince him that this was our best solution right now. We couldn't just sit around waiting for the police to do something – and we owed it to Steven at least to explore this idea. Finally, at his suggestion we talked to the hotel manager, who had been made aware of our situation by the embassy. He agreed to station guards outside our room and to call every fifteen minutes to check we were all right.

Although we felt reassured by this, I still spent a restless night, waking from time to time full of anxiety about what we might have let ourselves in for. At one point I woke and realised Alan wasn't next to me. I found him sitting in the bathroom, sobbing quietly.

'Alan, love, come back to bed,' I murmured, putting my arms around him. 'What is it?'

'He was my son too, you know.' I think the words came out louder than he had expected, and he startled me. 'I'm sorry, I've been trying to be so strong for you. I didn't mean you to wake up and find me.'

You're a selfish woman, Margaret, I told myself. Here you are, wallowing in your own misery, going on as if you're the only one who has been hurt. And all the while expecting Alan to support you and go along with all your hair-brained schemes. Of course he's grieving too. Of course he is feeling the pain of a father – he and Steven were closer than most fathers and sons I knew. It was as if I had been locked inside my own little bubble of sadness, and it suddenly popped. I wanted to share the grieving, and I wanted to try to help Alan through it. We lay down in bed and curled into one another like children.

'I tried not to replace his real dad,' he sobbed, 'I just wanted to be his best friend. Do you think he felt I was? He thought I was OK, didn't he?'

'Yes, love, he did. He loved you. You were always close. Don't you remember that time he said you were more of a dad than he could ever wish for?'

'Oh yes, yes I do. And he used to introduce us as his parents, didn't he?'

'Yes, which made you feel good, didn't it? And it made me feel good too.'

'We never had an argument or anything, we always talked about stuff. He was a good boy, wasn't he?'

'Yes, he never caused us any trouble. The girls were quite volatile, weren't they? I used to have loads of mother–daughter conflicts, but not with Steven.'

'Poor Steven,' Alan said.

'Poor Steven,' I echoed, quietly.

Eventually we fell into an exhausted sleep.

The next morning, rigid with nerves, we were waiting in our room when Paco and three strangers knocked at the door. I had rigged up my new voice recorder – not just to record our conversation, but to provide evidence should anything happen to us. Paco introduced them: Miguel from the office, a Filipino called Jose and a woman called Juliana. I scrutinised Jose's face – he looked more Hispanic than Asian. Filipino people have both races in their blood. Was this a face I could trust? He looked solemn, inscrutable, but he held my gaze. As they talked, we all started to relax a little. Jose and his wife Juliana lived in what we called 'the squatters' compound' in Angeles. This was where many locals lived – it was made up of a collection of run-down flats and public housing, with makeshift bamboo huts alongside the more permanent structures. Chickens and barefoot children scratched around in the dirt, men sat around smoking and eating, women washed and cooked outside. Large families shared small rooms, and I imagined that there were few secrets in the compound. I knew that some of Evelyn's relatives lived there too, and it was quite near Steven's house. This was a good start.

'Have you heard anything about this case already?' I asked.

'Yes, Ma'am,' said Juliana haltingly. 'I hear talk of Evelyn. She was very worry that Mr Steven want divorce. She said better husband dead than marry another woman and give new woman her money.' I nodded – this was all so believable – but could it just be gossip? 'I think this very bad, Ma'am. I hear Mr Steven dead, and I remember this. She not good Catholic girl. Many many people not happy about this killing.'

Jose, whose English was more fluent, said he had heard that Evelyn was moving house in a week's time. He also thought she was living part-time with her boyfriend. Again, this came as no surprise. After talking to them for nearly two hours, I knew this couple would be able to help us, and I felt I could trust them. I confided my suspicions and theories about Evelyn to them, and they agreed to do surveillance on Steven's house and find out what they could. 'Madam,' said Jose, 'we want to help you get justice for your son.' I was pleased with this, but I wasn't naïve enough to think this was their only motivation, and before they left I gave them money to hire a car and buy a camera. I also gave them the photofit picture from the police files. They were to report back to me daily.

'I need suspects, their names and addresses,' I repeated, as they took their leave of us.

Alone again in our hotel room, Alan and I hugged each other and grabbed a drink from the minibar. 'Well done, Marg,' said Alan, 'I think we'll look back on today and know you were right to put this in motion.' I was elated at his approval, and giddy with excitement – it felt as if something, finally, was going to happen and we were making it happen. Here I was, Margaret Davis from Bingham, behaving like Inspector Jane Tennison in *Prime Suspect*. I felt powerful, courageous, and at the same time very, very scared.

6
Money Talks

I had started the ball rolling, but I couldn't relax – not yet, not by a long chalk. I may have embarked on my own private investigation into my son's murder, but what was keeping me awake at night now was the children. I just couldn't get their wistful little faces out of my mind. Jessica, at three and a half, was a lively little girl with her mother's beauty and her father's happy-go-lucky nature. She had large brown eyes and silky black hair that she loved me to brush. Joshua was just a baby, with paler skin than his sister but with the same large dark eyes. I didn't know him as well as I knew Jessie, but I had been there at his birth and for his first few months of life. Steven had doted on them both, and each weekend when the maids were off duty he had taken on the lion's share of the childcare. Evelyn had always been happy for him to take charge of the shopping, cooking, feeding and even nappy-changing.

I vividly remembered that on one occasion we returned from a day's shopping to find two hungry children with an anxious maid, and nothing in the fridge except a cake we had been saving for a celebration later that night. The children had eaten half of it because there was no other food in the house. On another occasion Evelyn got upset that we were boiling up bones for the dog. 'The maids could eat that,' she said. I felt embarrassed, because it made us look wasteful, but I was horrified all the same. Another day we walked in and found Jessica at the table chewing on a fish head. Just the head, nothing else. If this was going on when we were there to observe, what on earth could be happening now no one was there? Who was ensuring that the children were being properly looked after?

I felt overwhelmed by a primeval need to encircle these two children with my arms and my love. They were just babies caught up in an evil, messy adult world – and I wanted to give them back their innocence, their joy, their freedom from sadness. I wanted to protect them, to heal them, to take them under my wings like a mother hen. What was their future now, without Steven? Would Evelyn let us come and visit them still? If it was true about her lover, what kind of a life would they have now? And if Evelyn was guilty, what then? All manner of horrible imaginings flashed in and out of my mind. I realised I had only a few days before Evelyn would be evicted by her landlady, and then goodness only knew where she might take them.

It was imperative that I speak to her and find out what her plans were, and if there might be any possibility of our taking the children for a holiday in England. It was surprising, and worrying, that she had not yet replied to my last phone message, in which I had asked if she needed any money.

Our lawyer, Christian Aguera, was in cautious mood when I called for his advice.

'I have been speaking to Sergeant Tampinco, who is in charge of your case. I gather you are being rather proactive.' I allowed myself a private smile. Little did he know just how proactive I was being. 'I must advise you to allow the authorities to do their job.' Huh, what job? I kept my cool, and decided not to tell him what I was up to on the investigation front.

'Of course,' I reassured him. 'My main priority now is deciding what to do about the children – in fact that is why I am calling. I think they need to get away from this situation and have a normal family life for a while. How can I get them passports and visas?' He considered this a moment, then suggested, 'You could perhaps offer their mother a few thousand pesos to allow you to have them for a few weeks. But if she refuses I think it would be best for you and your husband to return to the UK alone. You may also have to let her decide what to do about the body.'

'Thank you for your advice,' I replied levelly. He must be mad, I thought. *Buy* the children from her for a holiday, and if she says no just go back to the UK without Steven, and without his children? That was not what I wanted to happen, and I was becoming more confident about how to get things done here. As time would tell, though, the lawyer knew more about how things worked in his country than I did.

The next day I had an interesting call from Jose. 'Ma'am, I have talked to the auntie of Evelyn, her name Rosario Mabanglo. She knows many things, and will tell you these things, but first she needs some money.' Many things! This was it, I rejoiced, and called Reynoldo at the police station to let him know a witness was keen to talk if he could bring her to Makati from Angeles. He politely informed me that if I could get her to come to Makati then he would be prepared to talk to her. This made me angry: I had had it with this lack of responsiveness. Did I have to do everything myself?

'Come on Alan, we're going back to Angeles,' I announced. He nodded in a resigned fashion, and while he made the arrangements for a taxi and hotel, I confirmed with Jose that we would meet Rosario with him the following evening. There were other things I intended to do while we were there.

It was hard being back in Angeles, the city where we had once been so happy, and where now my beloved son lay cold and abandoned in a morgue a few blocks from our hotel. Every fibre of my body wanted to go and be with him that day, but I knew we could not leave our room for fear of being recognised by somebody who might report our presence to someone we'd rather remained ignorant of our whereabouts. I sat for hours just staring out of our window, watching the traffic, the street sellers, the dirty business of life going on in its familiar jaunty way. The room darkened with the approach of evening, and still I sat, mesmerised by the soft ebb and flow of the city. I felt as if I was being swept along on a dark tide of misery; there was no escaping, there would be no end.

The lights were just beginning to come on around the city when there was a call from reception to let me know that my guests had arrived. I roused myself and found my face wet with tears.

'I'll come down with you,' said Alan, waking from his nap and making a move towards the door.

'I think I'd better do this alone, love. It might be better woman to woman, you know.' I was anxious not to intimidate this elderly and probably ill-educated lady, and something told me that the more vulnerable I appeared, the more she might be prepared to tell me. So, heart in mouth, I walked to the foyer alone to meet Jose, Juliana and Rosario, Evelyn's aunt. In my bag was the voice recorder.

It was a difficult meeting. Jose acted as interpreter while Rosario spoke in a soft, faltering voice. She can't have been more than fiftysomething, but her face was as creased as an old apple. Small and birdlike, she sat twisting her hands in her lap, crying all the while. When she eventually started to talk, what she said was all over the place and I had to keep asking her to repeat things. I did feel, though, that she had felt respect and affection for Steven.

She told me he was a good man, a kind husband and father, and she believed that Evelyn felt that because she had married a wealthy man she could look down upon her impoverished relatives. There were some important pieces of information to come out of that meeting. Rosario told us that she often looked after Jessica while Evelyn met her boyfriend, whose name was Arnold Adoray. OK, so now we had a name. His wife had left him due to his relationship with Evelyn. Rosario had confronted Evelyn about the relationship, and the two had had an argument, during which Rosario had hit Evelyn in the face. 'Why are you doing this? You have a good, wealthy young husband at home,' she'd asked. Evelyn had replied that she loved him and they wanted to be together. Rosario told us that Evelyn always had plenty of money and used it to buy Arnold gifts. Aha, so that was where all Steven's money was going – of course – and he had thought it was to help Evelyn's family out! Rosario was fearful for Steven because Arnold had a reputation as a 'bad man'; she had shouted at Evelyn not to do anything bad to Steven. Rosario also spoke of Evelyn's sister Carmen, who lived with her and acted as nanny and maid. Carmen had fallen out with Evelyn because she believed Evelyn was planning to kill Steven. She had found this out because her husband Roberto used to work as a security guard with Arnold. OK, so there were people who knew something was being planned.

A boyfriend, a motive, a plan, and a witness. I could not believe what I was hearing. This meeting went on for over an hour, and I was having trouble controlling my anger. You knew he was going to die! I wanted to shout. You knew what they were planning, and yet you did nothing! You stupid, ignorant woman! Why didn't you warn Steven? Now here she was crying over photographs of him, hugging me, and crossing herself repeatedly. When I asked her to speak to the police, she shook her head and cried even harder. At length I realised I had to be conciliatory, so I hugged her, gave her money and thanked her for talking to me. Later that night I listened to the tape recording and typed up everything she had said. This would be for the police.

When she had left Jose explained that she would never go to the police with what she knew: it would be in effect an act of betrayal – her sister was Evelyn's mother. No one betrays their family in the Philippines. No, I thought bitterly, they just kill their husbands and get away with it. Still, she had been brave to come to me and tell me what she knew; this was useful information and I had to decide how best to use it.

'Back to Makati, then?' asked Alan when I returned to our room later that night.

'No, love. We're going to Evelyn's house tomorrow. I'm desperate to see the children, I want to talk to her and I'd like some things from Steven's room. Do you want to come too?'

'All right. It's gotta be done, I guess. I'll call Brian and ask him to come with us.'

We arrived at noon the following day. A maid we did not recognise answered the door, and backed off quickly when she saw the three of us. Evelyn appeared, clearly just having woken up, wearing a silk dressing gown and a nervous smile.

'Hello, Ma'am, Mr Alan. I was not expecting you.'

'We tried to call you, Evelyn, but there was no reply – is your phone working? I need to talk to you about the cremation, and I think the children need a holiday.'

'OK, I talk later.'

I nodded. 'Are the children here?'

'Yes, they are out the back with the maids.'

First things first – I hurried to see them, and Jessie immediately rushed into my arms. 'Nana, my nana!' Her little face was one big smile. 'Come and see my new dolly.' We sat and played with her for a while. Joshua was crawling on the floor wearing just a vest, and one of the maids was tailing him, attempting to feed him pieces of banana. I could never get used to this practice of feeding children on the hop.

Structured mealtimes were what I believed in. Still, this wasn't the time or place to worry about that. The main thing was they seemed to be healthy, if a bit thin and grubby. I left Alan with them after an hour or so and went into Steven's study.

Immediately I knew it had been tampered with. I knew that room like my own: I knew my way around his computer; I knew where his private files and work files were kept. Like me, he kept and filed everything: receipts, ticket stubs, concert programmes, household bills, restaurant menus, prescription forms . . . everything. It broke my heart to sit at his desk and know that this was where he had been sitting the last time we had spoken. I spent some time sifting through his files. I particularly wanted to find the share certificates Steven and I jointly owned in his software company. They were missing.

'I have them in safekeeping and I will give them to my lawyer,' claimed Evelyn when I asked her where they were. I decided not to press the issue, and a few moments later she left the house quietly without saying goodbye. I cursed her under my breath, as I had not yet had a chance to get an answer on the cremation or about the children. How stupid of me not to pin her down while I had the chance. While she was gone Alan and I hurriedly packed up everything else from Steven's room that I thought might be useful. She wasn't going to have any of it, even if it turned out to be rubbish. I took papers, files, boxes of personal items and letters of gratitude from the charities he supported. I downloaded files from his hard disk and removed his floppy disks. It felt like a violation of his privacy, but it also felt as if I was helping him, doing him a service in some way – clearing up his room as I had done countless times when he was a teenager.

Then in the drawer of his desk I found something that made my heart miss a beat. A pawn receipt for a wedding ring, signed by Evelyn – dated two weeks before Steven died. No wonder he had been angry with her. Had this been the last straw, I wondered, and remembered with a lurch that the last time I spoke to him he had told me she had 'pushed me too far this time'. I had asked him if he wanted me to come over. 'Only if you've got nothing else to do,' he had replied. Was that a cry for help? If only I had realised. I think I laughed it off at the time, saying I'd see him anyway in September. This would play on my mind for weeks. I should have gone out to him. If only, if only. Why didn't I see this coming? Still, I pocketed the receipt. More damning evidence.

The last thing I found was a tiny box. In it was Steven's wedding ring, engraved by Evelyn with the words *My love Evelyn*. Why had he put it in this box? Why was he not wearing it? Had he taken it off in a fit of rage? I had so many questions I wanted to ask him . . .

After hugging the children and promising to see them again soon, we loaded the boxes into the car and drove away, a tearful Jessie waving at us from the front porch. How I hated leaving them. I wanted to check into an Angeles hotel and go back to see them and their mother the next day, but Alan persuaded me to return to Makati.

'Let's go through Steve's things first, we only scratched the surface this afternoon. You never know, we might find something useful. And we need to check in with the police. We can come back to Angeles at the drop of a hat.' And so we took all the boxes to Steven's office, knowing we could not keep all his stuff, reading and sorting and deciding what to throw away. It was so sad, looking at all the insignificant paraphernalia that's left behind after a life is over, things of no importance to anyone except Steven. Not even his children would want his phone bills, but he had carefully kept everything.

And actually, thank goodness he did. I knew that if there was anything useful to be found it would be here. Their marriage certificate, for example. Instead of printing her name as Evelyn Talagolgon, she was listed as Danita Talagolgon. 'Look, Alan, her name isn't even on the certificate. She's given a false name. Perhaps this means they weren't officially married?'

'Don't jump to conclusions,' he laughed. 'Evelyn is probably her nickname, or her middle name, or something. Not all people use their given names. Look – here's her birth certificate, Danita Talagolgon, born on 10 January 1977. That would make her 21 when she married, just like she said. She wouldn't have someone else's birth certificate, would she?' I wasn't convinced by this, and stored the information away. Before long, the truth would emerge.

I remembered their wedding day so clearly. I was so excited for Steven, and so thrilled that he'd saved getting married for when we were on holiday with him – he was a great one for springing surprises on me. That morning I had gone out and bought Evelyn a lovely posy of flowers. I gave them to her in their high-rise apartment. She looked stunning in a white suit with all her shiny black hair and her flawless skin, and the pink and white roses would complete the look. But she took the flowers and dumped them in the kitchen. 'Aren't you taking them with you?' I asked. 'No, I'll have them later,' she replied. Keep a low profile, Margaret, I told myself. Don't fuss. It's a cultural thing. I had bought her a gold bracelet with little stars and flowers on it as a wedding present, so I decided to hang on to that too. I'm not having that left in the kitchen as well, I thought. I never did give it to her, even though we went off on honeymoon with them. Somehow I never got the opportunity.

We did make one very important discovery that day. Footage from the security camera at Steven's home – miles of film showing visitors entering and leaving the house. We turned this over to the police immediately, and a couple of days later when we called in at the police station we were welcomed enthusiastically.

'Good afternoon, Mrs Davis Ma'am,' said Ramon Tampinco happily. 'We have some news for you.' About bloody time, I thought.

It appeared that they had shown the spy-cam footage to a local security guard who had identified a face he recognised – that of Roberto Palabay, a name I knew. He was married to Evelyn's sister Carmen, who worked for a time as her maid. Mama Rosario had mentioned that this sister knew something. The police had questioned Roberto, who acted as if he had been expecting them. 'Ma'am, this man he shake all through the interview, but he say he know nothing. We think he know something but he not telling.' They had also interviewed Evelyn's landlady, who was complimentary about Steven but had nothing but complaints to make about Evelyn, her rowdy friends and her poor record with paying rent. Finally, they had talked to the neighbours who had mentioned seeing Evelyn on the back of a motorbike with a man who was not her husband. So my financial sweetener to the police had paid off.

I told the officer I had a witness who had confirmed that Evelyn had been having an affair, and up to two witnesses who knew Evelyn had wanted to harm Steven. I had also been given the name of the boyfriend. The policeman looked at me long and hard.

'Who is this witness?'

I explained who she was, and pulled the transcript of our conversation out of my bag. 'You must interview her.'

'This is not possible.'

'Please,' I begged. 'Please – she has vital information about the plot to kill my son. I need you to talk to her.'

'I must discuss this with my superiors,' he eventually said. 'Maybe we can do something. Write down what you want me to ask her and I will see what we can do.' He looked unsettled.

OK, I thought, a little unorthodox, but if that was what it was going to take, then fine. I nodded and squeezed Alan's hand – this had to be progress at last. We thanked him profusely and left. Back at the hotel there was more good news: Mrs Galang from the funeral parlour had called to say Evelyn had agreed to a cremation a few days later. Alan and I allowed ourselves a small celebration that night. These two things – a decent investigation and a cremation – we would have regarded as our basic rights back home, yet here we had had to fight tooth and nail for them.

I knew my next job was to persuade Rosario to talk to the police. Jose had been adamant that she would never betray her family, but I called him anyway and spent half an hour pressurising him to ask her. He was doubtful. 'Rosario, she old and sick, she need money for medicine and food, she not well, she not want to come long way to Makati.' Each excuse I waved away with a promise to pay, provide food, book a taxi. Eventually he agreed to try, and I called in at the station with a list of questions for Reynoldo in the event that she might turn up.

The next day, to our surprise and delight, Rosario arrived at our hotel with three elderly companions. She stumbled as she emerged from the cab, and I noticed she was sweating profusely. Perhaps she really was ill – oh God, I prayed silently, please let her hold up for this. Jose asked if I could feed them, and we all trooped into a dingy corner café where I provided them all with rice, steamed vegetables, and the popular local dish chicken adobo. It took forever, and it was late afternoon by the time I got them all to the police station.

We sat for six hours in the homicide interview room – the

one with the 1930s typewriter – Reynoldo asking the frail old lady my questions and one-finger-typing the answers painstakingly onto a wafer-thin sheet of paper. I watched Rosario throughout, willing her to give the police enough information, smiling and nodding encouragement. Of course it was all in the local language, Tagalog, and I could only make out a few words. When it was all over she looked exhausted, so I fed her and her companions again and put them in a taxi back to Angeles. As I thanked her I pressed a wad of notes into her bony hand. 'For your trouble,' I whispered. 'Graçias.'

I immediately called Reynoldo to ask him what he thought of this new evidence. Surely this was the break they had been waiting for?

'All this information is still circumstantial,' he answered. 'It is not enough to require Evelyn to come in for an interview. I'm sorry.'

My head sank onto my chest and hot tears sprang to my eyes. All the effort of taping the old lady, of persuading her to talk to the police, of paying her and Jose a fortune to come here today, of spending a whole day doing everything I could to ensure it all ran smoothly – all for nothing. Nothing. I felt I had done as much as anyone could do, and more than most people would even think of doing. Alan sat in disbelieving silence, his arm round my shoulder, as I sobbed with impotent rage. On top of it all, the next day was Steven's cremation. I needed to be strong for that, and I needed to plan how to approach Evelyn. When I managed to stop crying I looked at my bundle of papers on Steven's case.

'What's the form, then, Margaret?' Alan asked. 'We'll have to be up and out early to get there in good time.'

'I'll be in a right state tomorrow, I know that already. Let me think. This is Steven's cremation, it's not a rehearsal, it's our last chance to see him. Can you take photos? Take loads.

We can always delete distressing ones, but we'll never be able to go back.' Was this a sick thing to want? I didn't know, I just wanted to hang on to his earthly image and have as much to remember him by as possible. Already the thought that his body was to be burnt to a cinder tomorrow was making me tremble.

'We must take his ashes with us, so don't let me leave without them. God knows what it's going to cost to get them, but we should take cash just in case.'

Alan nodded grimly. 'What about the children?'

'Here are the passport forms that I got from the embassy weeks ago. I've filled them in, and all I need is Evelyn's signature.'

'How are you going to do that? She's not daft. She'll think you want to take her kids away from her.' Alan and I hadn't discussed this fully, and I sensed he was worried that I wanted to snatch the children from Evelyn. Typical Alan, not confronting me directly over this.

'Look, she's the mother, and if she's innocent it's her right to look after her children. I don't have a problem with that. All I want to do is to take them for a holiday, in this country if necessary, until all this blows over. It's also important for them to have passports to give them an identity: if we left it up to her they'd never get one. I hope I can persuade her of that.'

'I still don't think Steven's cremation is either the time or place to deal with things like this.'

'Look.' I was getting angry. 'I've got to take every opportunity that I get. If I haven't even got the forms in my bag . . .' Alan nodded his agreement. Clearly he did not want to discuss this further.

I felt sick and nervous at the thought of the next day: I knew it was going to be one of the hardest days of my life.

7
The Final Goodbye

We were on holiday somewhere – it looked like an English seaside resort with a pebbly beach and a windswept promenade. The girls were there, and Steven's dad Joe, and Steven. The children were all small, with swimsuits on. Laughing, running in and out of the water hand in hand. Jumping over the waves as they broke on the shore, splashing each other and sitting down delightedly in the foam. As I watched, Steven turned to me and waved. He was saying something but I couldn't make it out. Then he started walking out to sea. He didn't stop, and the water was getting deeper. I got up to run to him, but my legs wouldn't work. I shouted out, but my voice was mute. No one else had noticed; only I saw his figure gradually getting smaller. I gestured frantically to the others, but they carried on jumping over the waves. The water was up to his neck; in a moment it would engulf him. There was nothing I could do.

I woke with a start. It was a grey dawn, the day of Steven's cremation. For a while the Kodachrome colours of my dream stayed with me, and with them the image of my son waving at me for the last time. Such a dear little boy, with his stripy swimming trunks and blond sticky-up hair. I wasn't ready to say goodbye to him. There was so much I had never said. There was no justice in a world that could wrench such a boy from his mother. The looming events of this day weighed on my chest like a heavy, dull ache. Dear God, how was I to get through it? Alan stirred next to me, and I reached for his hand. Suddenly my mind filled with everything I should have done: I should have insisted on taking his body back home, he should be cremated on English soil, not in this God-forsaken country. His family should be here with him – why had I not flown the girls over for a proper funeral? How can they face the reality of his death, how can they ever get over it if they have not had a chance to say goodbye to him? And I wanted to share my grief and feel the support of my family today. I needed not to feel alone. My body shook with explosive sobs and Alan could do nothing to console me.

Eventually the alarm clock rang, and I knew I had to pull myself together. Try not to think about it, Margaret, I told myself. Don't think about Steven, don't think about what you should have done. Don't think about the day he was born, how he was as a baby, a boy, a young man. Don't think about how he died, don't try to imagine his last moments. Don't think about what is going to happen to his body today. Don't think about how his sisters and his children are going to cope with this. Just do what you have to do. I mentally went through my list: get up, shower, dress, eat breakfast, collect my documents, take taxi to the funeral parlour in Angeles. Come back here when it is all over. Put like that it sounded almost easy.

When we arrived at the funeral parlour there was no one about, so we sat and waited on a bench outside. The road was busy and street sellers were hawking their wares. People walked past us, giving us curious stares. We sat in a meditative silence. I felt still and detached. Calm, even. Then a white van drew up and a small child jumped out and ran into my arms. It was Jessica, and she hugged me excitedly, clearly imagining this was a fun day out. Had no one explained to her what was to happen today? She was nearly four, old enough to understand a little. 'Do you know why we are here, Jessie?' I asked. She shook her head, eyes bright and eager, as if expecting a treat. More people emerged from the van – one of Evelyn's sisters, carrying Joshua, another sister, Carmen, and others I did not recognise. Then Evelyn walked towards me, and with a brief 'Hello, Ma'am' she passed by and went into the waiting room inside. I turned back to Jessica.

'We have come to say goodbye to your daddy. You won't see him again, he is going to Heaven to be with the angels.'

'What will he do there? Why can't he stay with me?'

Oh Jesus. 'He wanted to stay with you, darling, but he couldn't. He will be looking down on you though, and watching over you, and seeing you grow up into a beautiful, kind girl.'

'I miss my daddy, Nana,' Jessica whispered. Tears suddenly filled her eyes. Oh no, had I done the right thing? Had I told her too much? 'I miss him too,' I replied gently. 'But we'll never forget him, will we?

'Look.' I reached into my bag to deflect more tears. 'I have a present for you.' With tears in my eyes I fastened a silver necklace with a heart-shaped pendant around her neck. It was engraved with the words *I love you*.

I wanted Jessica to have something from me in case I never saw her again.

'It's pretty, Nana.' She smiled as I wiped her eyes.

A young woman came out to look for Jessica. 'I am Danita, Evelyn's older sister,' she said to me. 'Shall we go in, Jessie?' She took Jessica's small hand, and I followed them into the funeral parlour with Alan. Aha, my brain ticked over. So the mystery of the name on the marriage certificate was solved – Evelyn must have used her identity. But why? 'How much older than Evelyn are you?' I asked.

'Four years,' she replied, with surprise at such a question on such a day. Then it dawned on me. This meant that Evelyn was only seventeen – underage, in law – when she married poor, duped Steven. And only fourteen when they first met. Hardly had I absorbed this shocking realisation than I saw her inside in the gloom.

'How are you, Evelyn?' I approached her with what I hoped was a kind smile.

Her expression was cold. 'We are well, but I need money for food and a new house. I cannot stay there, I have too many memories and I am disturbed.'

Before I could reply the hearse drew up outside, and as if from nowhere staff appeared in order to carry Steven's casket into the chapel. I felt Alan's hand steadying my elbow and we all trooped into the chapel behind Steven. I thought perhaps Evelyn might go towards the casket, but she made no move to do so. She wasn't going to get away with that.

'Let's go together, Evelyn,' I said, taking her hand. She drew back reluctantly, but I was firm. We looked down at him together, and I saw through my tears that his skin had taken on a waxy pallor. My son, I breathed silently, my heart hammering. My son. Evelyn regarded his face, dry-eyed and expressionless. Then I remembered something I had read in one of the books on Filipino beliefs, and took a gamble.

'Look at his fists – they are clenched. Steven is angry, Evelyn, his spirit will not rest until his killers are in jail. He knows who they are, he's waiting for justice.' I heard her draw in a small but perceptible gasp, and I put my arm around her in a comforting fashion. She was shaking like a leaf.

'I must go to baby Joshua,' she said suddenly, pulling away from me.

We sat for a while listening to piped music, then the attendants arrived to take the casket away. No smooth mechanism to glide the coffin away, no subtle drawing of a velour curtain as there would be back home, no sanitised, dignified exit; here the coffin was hoisted up and carried into the next room, where I could hear the furnace roaring. I rushed after my son's body but was gently restrained by the owner of the funeral parlour.

'Please, Mrs Galang,' I begged, 'I want to hold my son after you have taken him from the casket, I need to touch him one more time.'

I was surprised to see her eyes fill with tears, but she nodded professionally. Her empathy touched me, and I began to cry hysterically, full of fear for what I would see, wondering whether his body would be black and blue – it was three weeks since I had seen him properly. The skin on my face felt so tight I thought it would crack, and my heart was racing – this was the moment I had been dreading. I took a deep breath and went back to where Evelyn was sitting. 'Come, let's say goodbye together,' I managed to say. I led her by the hand into a large room. It had a dirty floor, and grubby off-white ceramic tiles on the wall. Devoid of furniture and windows, it was dominated by a large tin oven. The doors were open. We were not supposed to be in here.

Steven was laid on a bare metal trolley, feet facing the oven. He was still wearing the same suit he was dressed in when we saw him last. I undid the laces on one of his shoes, and motioned Evelyn to do the same. Shaking off my fear, I cupped his head in my hands, and kissed his dear cold face goodbye. How I had loved him and cradled his small body as a baby, with so much joy and hope. In death I loved him so much I could almost hear his voice – were his lips moving? I grabbed his whole body fiercely, aching to restore him to life. I shook him and hugged him as tightly as I could, never wanting to let go. But there was no give in his body at all – he was frozen hard. The cold went right through me like an electric shock. If I could have breathed life into my son I would truly have changed places then and there. Then I reached out for Evelyn – she was pale, and crying for the first time. She is only small, is Evelyn, and – my heart bursting with grief, rage and something close to insanity – I pushed her forward onto Steven's body, forcing her arms around him and pinning her there with my own body. I could feel the strength leaving her, and I was suddenly afraid she would faint.

'Swear to me you had nothing to do with this,' I whispered.

'I swear, Ma'am, I swear on my kids' life and my mother's life. I love Stayban, I love my husband, I am so sad, Ma'am.' With that she sank to the floor, sobbing. I felt a pang of pity for this ignorant girl. How I wished I could see into her heart. What was the real truth? Was she still dissembling, even here – in front of her dead husband? I desperately wanted to believe she was innocent.

It was time for me to perform my last act for my son. 'Do this with me, Evelyn,' I said, pulling her to her feet. Taking a deep breath, and mouthing our private prayers for his soul, we pushed the trolley into the oven. His body was to be burnt, and with it a part of me would also be destroyed. The oven door clanged shut with a terrible finality. Goodbye, my beloved son.

I looked at his shoes, sitting on the side where we had left them. These mundane items still held the creases and folds, the imprint of his living feet; and there they now stood, looking forlorn and lost. An unbearable wave of sadness washed over me.

Afterwards Alan and I sat outside on the bench, waiting for Steven's ashes – knowing that it could take hours. During the rainy season in the Philippines, the heat does not diminish but the humidity rises, and we were clammy and sweaty. Suddenly we were startled by a loud crash of thunder, the heavens opened, and thick dark rain fell in heavy torrents. We looked up at the blackened sky. How appropriate, I thought – angry, depressing weather.

'Steve's on his way,' commented Alan wryly, as people made their way back inside to shelter.

There was no let-up in the rain for a long time, and the children were becoming restless. Gradually people started to chat quietly, and I saw my opportunity to have a talk with Evelyn, thinking that we had both calmed down since the ugly confrontation over Steven's body two hours earlier. Drawing her into a side room, I hugged her as warmly as I was able to and asked her how she was coping. She talked of her sadness, and her need to move house for the children and to distance herself from unhappy memories. She did not know I knew she was being evicted.

'I have seen a nice house with garden for the kids,' she said, probably knowing I would approve of this notion.

'Where is it?'

'I don't know, Ma'am, it is in Marisol somewhere.' This was the same district as her current house.

'What is the address? Have you been there?'

'I went yesterday but I don't know address, when I move I send you address. But now I need money for rent and deposit.'

'How much?'

'About 30,000 pesos.' This was about £300. I told her I did not have that much on me; she would have to meet me later. She clearly did not want me to know where she was going with the children, but I would ignore this for now. I took a deep breath.

'I would like to take the children for a holiday – and you too, if you like.' There, I had said it.

'No, Ma'am, I must stay here, and I could not be without my kids. To wake in the morning with no husband and no children, I would have nothing.' I could hear fear in her voice. I needed to try another tack.

'Steven has money in the UK that belongs to you,' I lied.

'Really?' She smiled at last. Then: 'When will I get it? You know I have nothing, and I need to buy food and things for the kids.'

'It's a little difficult – I need you to come with me to get the insurance money, and there is a house too. You will be very wealthy.' I was playing all my cards, false though they were. I hated being this devious, but it could be my last chance to help the children. I felt so strongly that they needed a period of normal family life. If I couldn't offer it to them, what kind of a grandmother was I? I continued, 'They will need evidence that Steven had dependents, a wife and children. In fact I have some forms here to sign to prove that he had a family here.' I drew out the passport forms.

'You have birth certificates, that is enough,' Evelyn said. Good point, I thought. You're not that stupid then.

'They don't have your signature on them,' I replied, thinking quickly. She looked unsure, so I drew out my purse. 'I may have a little money to give you now,' I said, pulling out about £60 in notes. 'If you sign these forms you may have this money.' I could see her internal struggle – she wanted the money badly.

'You won't take my kids, Ma'am. I could not live without my kids.'

'Of course I won't take your children, Evelyn. I just want to give them a holiday.' And I meant it with all my heart. If she was innocent, of course she would keep her children. 'While you are able to look after them, I will support you and give you money. These children are important to me, and so are you. You are Steven's wife, and I know how much he loved you. I have no desire to take your children away from you. They need their mother.' And their father, I thought bitterly. We had been in the room for about three hours, and I could hear movement in the other room. Perhaps the ashes were ready. I knew time was running out.

'Please sign here, Evelyn.' I passed her the pen and indicated where she should sign. *Evelyn Davis*, she wrote, somewhat painstakingly. I looked at it. 'Is that right? On your marriage certificate it says your first name is Danita, not Evelyn.' She looked shocked, as if I had caught her nicking sweets.

'It's OK, Ma'am, this is how it is.' I wasn't born yesterday, love, I thought – but I nodded as if convinced, and handed her the money. Another nail in her coffin, as far as I was concerned. But she had signed the forms, that was what mattered. She looked at the wad of notes and then uttered a truly shocking statement: 'My children are worth more than this. If you want them you will need to give me much more money.' So much for her not being able to live without her kids. 'I need two hundred thousand peso.' My God, she was asking for £2000.

'Evelyn, I do not want to buy your children. They are my grandchildren and I love them, but they are your children. You are their mother.' I stopped short of expressing my horror that she would contemplate selling them – maybe I had misunderstood, but I remembered something Brian had said about Filipina girls who have children by Western men in order to accumulate wealth. I didn't believe him at the time, but here was my own daughter-in-law attempting to barter her children for cash. I felt sick to my stomach.

Heavy-hearted, I went back to join Alan in the waiting room, but my eyes were distracted by a terrible sight. The doors to the furnace room were open, and there lay my son on the trolley. Except it wasn't Steven as I knew him, it was his skeleton – just ash and bone. I had no idea this was what happened after a body was cremated. I imagined he would just disintegrate into a pile of anonymous grey ashes, not be lying there in his fully-grown form. I held my breath, not knowing what to do, appalled. I couldn't even cry. This was my son, beyond flesh. Suddenly Alan was there, drawing me away – shocked, and shaking just as I was.

Much later, it seemed, a staff member appeared with a large jug containing the kind of ashes I had expected to see, but now I was imagining him having crushed up Steven's skeleton with a hammer. He casually poured the contents of the jug into a plastic bag, placed the bag in a small white box, secured the lid, and handed the box to Evelyn. *No!*

She hugged it closely to her. 'My husband,' she wailed, doing a good imitation of a grief-stricken wife. Perhaps this was the first time she had realised that he was really dead.

'Please hand the ashes over,' ordered Mrs Galang. 'We have an agreement.'

'I cannot, this is my Stayban, I love him so much.' She gripped the box so tightly I could see her knuckles whiten. Everyone was looking now, and she was certainly giving a good performance. I didn't know what to do – I had to have the ashes.

'Please, Evelyn,' I said. She shook her head, her eyes fierce and defiant.

'Mama?' Jessica was pulling at Evelyn's skirt, only to be brushed aside. The little girl ran to me.

'What's wrong, Nana?' she asked tearfully. What a dreadful scene for this child to witness.

'Nothing, sweetheart,' I managed to say. 'It's just that we are all sad about your daddy.'

'You have your son, you must give Margaret hers,' said Mrs Galang eventually, taking the box firmly from Evelyn.

My hands closed around the warm box of ashes. At last I had my beloved son once again in my arms.

8
Results At Last

Back in Makati the rain fell relentlessly, as it always did during this season. Instead of the streets being washed clean by the downpours, it seemed to me that they were getting dirtier and muddier. The gutters ran with brown water, full of rubbish – food wrappers, bones, cigarette ends. Steven used to say he loved the rain, he found it exhilarating and refreshing. For me it was all part of the chaos and frustration of this country: the rain would stop in its own good time, and the authorities would get things done in theirs. Meanwhile there was nothing we could do but wait. We were confined to the hotel, and still had the armed security guards outside our room.

The day after the cremation we received a strange email from Evelyn:

From: Evelyn Davis
To: Margaret Davis
Date: 14 August 2002

I hope you guys are well since weather is not too good. Thank you for the long talk we had yesterday, I felt your motherly love towards us, it was good to ask what we can do to solve the problem and what else we can make to process everything in peaceful way and hand in hand helping each other. Without knowing it we had a dispute already in our heart though we don't meant it. I would like to tell you that I don't have any hurt feelings towards you and that I love you as Steven loves you too.

Whatever I have done wrong without my knowledge that hurts you, I don't really meant it. And so from now on I promise my self to listen first to you because I know you won't leave us alone and I will learn a lot from you. For all of it sorry for the misunderstanding from the past. I will be there tomorrow to see you but I cannot bring the kids, it is not good for them to travel when the weather is not good. Jessica miss you guys a lot. Evelyn.

We didn't know quite what to make of this. It sounded like an apology, an olive branch of sorts, and part of me started to feel sorry for her. Perhaps I had got her wrong – was she just a simple girl from the provinces trying to do her best? Or was it a cynical heartstring-pulling exercise to keep the money flowing? I wondered who helped her send it, and what she was hoping to achieve. I had agreed to meet her the following day to hand over the rest of the passport cash, but I was disappointed that she was not bringing the children – and the weather did not seem a good enough excuse. She was right about one thing though: I wasn't about to leave them alone.

In the event the next day brought interesting news from our informant Jose. One of the photographs he had taken while on surveillance outside Evelyn's house was of a man who seemed to resemble the photofit picture we had given him from the police files. According to his sources, this person was a security guard at the airbase. When Martin saw the photo he let out a long, low whistle. 'This is definitely one of the gunmen,' he confirmed. 'It's a dead ringer.' Halleluja. We passed this information on to the police who, bless them, acted immediately and went to Angeles to find the man. His name was Alex Dagami, and on duty with him at the airbase at the same time was Roberto Palabay, whom the police had already interviewed. They arrested both men, but later let Palabay go, owing to lack of evidence. They would have a long time to regret this.

On the same day, Martin was sitting in his office in Angeles, waiting for news from the police. His office was directly opposite the police station, and at that time he was spending much of his time staring out of the window, thinking about Steve. That morning he saw the police bringing Dagami into the station: he jumped up and rushed across the road.

'That's the bastard who killed my friend!' he yelled. Paco had followed him, and told me that Martin was distraught, very traumatised. Dagami merely said coldly, 'I have never seen this man.' A little later Dagami's supervisor arrived at the police station from the airbase to see what had happened to his subordinate. Martin went crazy.

'That's him! That's the other one! This is the man who put the gun to my head.'

The police were surprised, and according to Paco tried to calm him down. 'Are you sure?' they asked.

'Definitely,' said Martin. 'I recognise his eyes.' That was not enough for the police. They must have decided that Martin was too upset to think clearly, and allowed the supervisor to return to his work. Martin told me later that he had a hard time convincing the police to go back to the airbase to arrest the man. When they finally did, the following day, his gun was not in his holster. They arrested him on suspicion of murder. His name? Arnold Adoray, the man Rosario had claimed was having an affair with Evelyn.

We could hardly believe our ears when Reynoldo phoned to give us this news. Two of the main suspects under arrest at last! Catherine was thrilled when I called:

'Mum – that's great! It can only be a matter of time before someone lets on that Ev had something to do with it. What are they charged with?'

'Murder One it's called. The sentence for that is life, and over here life means life – or 40 years, anyway which is life for most people – so they will suffer in a squalid stinking hole of a jail for ever.'

'Only 40 years? That's not what I call life and it's still too good for them. Why did they let the third one go?'

'Not enough evidence. Maybe it was someone else.'

'But what about Evelyn?'

'Again, still not enough evidence, apparently, not even enough to question her. But you know me, I'm working on it.'

'What about the kids? I bet Jessica and Josh are having a rough time.'

'I've got passport forms for them but she wants £2000.'

'Get her arrested and you'll get the kids for free,' was Cathy's cynical response – but I knew I couldn't bank on that. After speaking to a few more delighted family members and friends, I realised I had a phone message from Evelyn, who I was supposed to be meeting later that day. She asked if she could see me the following day instead – she had something to tell me. Aha! Was this going to be a confession? I wondered what she would do now two of the men were in custody. I called her back to ask her to meet me in Steven's Makati offices: I did not want to be alone with her, just in case. I got the police to agree to be there too.

Evelyn turned up at the appointed hour, accompanied by her now habitual entourage of friends. She had the children with her, thank goodness, and Alan took them off for a walk while her friends waited in reception and I sat down with her in Steven's old office. It was so full of Steven still: photos on the walls of him with his family, flying certificates, a painting of the island of Cebu I'd bought him after our last holiday there. I stared at it and remembered how distant Evelyn had been during those two weeks – it was just after that awful miscarriage and at the time I put her moodiness down to losing the baby, hormones and what have you. But thinking back, she was on her mobile more often than not, texting and giggling with some friend or relative, but sullen and unresponsive with us. Even now Alan always holds my hand wherever we go, but I noticed how Evelyn would shrug Steve's arm off her shoulder, wriggle out of his embrace. Just subtle little touches, but things that mums notice. In fact Alan said at the time, 'She's probably got another chap on the end of that phone,' and I pooh-poohed him. Now I realised he had been right: she must have been conducting an affair under Steven's very nose.

Evelyn was snivelling about having no money and no husband. I listened to her for a while, wondering when she was going to tell me whatever she had on her mind. Eventually I asked her, 'What did you want to tell me, Evelyn?'

'All this what I say, Ma'am. I am so unhappy, I don't know what to do now.' She launched into another round of complaints – everything was wrong: the house, her family, the children, the police, the weather . . .

'Do you know that the police have arrested two men?' It was time to push her.

'Yes, Ma'am, I will go to the jail to talk to the police. I want to know what happened to my husband and why these bad men do such things.' Yeah, right. She wants to see her boyfriend.

'I'll come with you.'

'No, Ma'am, I do this alone. I need to talk to the police about everything.' Well, if she wasn't going to confess to me was she going to confess to the police? There was a chance, I thought. The door swung ajar, and I saw her friends watching us silently from the reception area. I felt uncomfortable, a little afraid, and very vulnerable. A moment later the police arrived, as promised. I was relieved to see them, but Evelyn immediately stood up, a look on her face like that of a frightened animal. Or was this my imagination? At the same moment Alan returned with the children, Joshua in a buggy and Jessica clinging to his neck.

'Can we have the children to stay with us for a few days in our hotel?' he asked. 'They look so tired, it will do them good to spend some time with us before we have to leave.' Evelyn looked unsure, and asked where we were staying. Alan sensibly gave her the name of a fictitious hotel – we did not want any uninvited guests. She looked at Jessica, and shook her head.

'Please Mama, please,' Jessica cried. Reluctantly Evelyn agreed to our having her, but said Joshua needed to stay at home as he was teething. The usual excuse, but we acquiesced, and agreed to hand Jessica back the following Monday.

While we gathered Jessica's things, I heard Tampinco say to Evelyn, 'We would like to invite you to the station to discuss your husband's death.' She nodded meekly. 'I will come this afternoon.' Fantastic! At last.

'Come on Jessie, say goodbye to Mummy – you're coming with Nana and Alan for a little while, we're going to have some fun together.' I took her to hug Evelyn, who was silent and wide-eyed, perhaps afraid of the police.

'Bye bye Mama. Bye bye baby Joshua.' She rushed over to Evelyn's sister, who was jiggling the ten-month-old on her knee.

'I'm hungry, Nana,' said Jessica as we left. I looked at her – she seemed paler than usual, and thin, and was shivering a little despite the warm afternoon air. I picked her up and gave her a big cuddle. 'Tell you what. Shall we go and have some chicken and rice, and then shall we get you some new clothes and a nightie and a swimming costume, and then shall we go for a swim in our lovely pool?' She nodded happily as I set her down, and we walked off to a local restaurant, hand in hand.

'That should have tired her out good and proper,' re-marked Alan later that evening, as we settled Jessica into bed – we thought it would be best for her to be in our bed with us for comfort. It was true, she was completely exhausted, but she was determined to keep herself awake until we went to bed, watching us constantly with her big brown eyes as if we would disappear if she closed them, and refusing to have the light turned out. When I lay down beside her, she slipped her small soft hand into mine and gripped it tightly. From time to time during the night I tried to release her grip in order to turn over or to get a bit more comfortable, but each time I let go she woke up and cried. I realised how badly she needed reassurance and love, and my heart bled for this little thing who at three and a half had been through so much.

The next morning we arrived at the police station to find some very satisfied-looking officers, and the two suspects chained together and about to be charged. I could hardly bear to look at these men, but one of the officers asked me to accompany them to the courtroom. Were these really my son's murderers? I finally looked at them, expecting to see something unusual – wicked eyes or some kind of brooding expression. But they both looked like fairly average Filipino guys. I was surprised at how young they seemed. While I watched, they were formally charged with the murder by the officer who had led me in. One of them – I later found out this was Alex Dagami – cried out, 'I am innocent, Ma'am!' The other, Arnold Adoray, hung his head and wept. 'I'm sorry,' I thought I heard him say.

'Do you have mothers?' I asked them. They both nodded. 'Well, your mothers will know the pain of losing their sons. My son is dead, and when you are in jail you too will be lost to your mothers. They will feel that you are dead.' I was bitter and deeply angry, but my rage prevented me from saying more. And yet I felt unbearably sad too. Three lives cut short by utter stupidity. Could Evelyn really be responsible for this mess? Could she really have given the orders to murder her husband?

Alan was waiting with Jessica back in the interview room, and we asked the officer how the interview with Evelyn had gone. There had been an article in that morning's *Philstar*, entitled *Pinay wife tagged in Briton slay case?* The wording was odd but it was clear what it meant. I waved it at the police – it talked about 'the possible involvement of his Filipina wife and her alleged lover'.

'What did she have to say for herself, then?' I challenged him, 'when you interviewed her yesterday?'

'She didn't turn up.'

'Then go and get her!' I said before I had time to control my tongue. It was so hard not to be angry and over-assertive with these officers – they were probably doing what they could. He looked offended, and turned away from me. Shit, I thought, I've lost his goodwill. I'd forgotten they don't like to be told what to do.

'Please try to contact her,' cut in Alan. 'I'm sure she has information you need.'

'We will do what we can. She informed us she was unwell.' The response was curt. My God, he is going to let her go free, I thought. We must find more evidence against her.

Suddenly Jessica cried out in fear, and hid behind me: she had caught sight of the two accused men being led back to the holding cell.

'Do you know these people?' I asked her gently.

'Yes,' she whispered.

Jessica calmed down a little after we got her out of the police station, but she was obviously no longer the happy little girl that I remembered from our regular visits. I knew we had to get her away and into a happier environment. For the moment, this was our hotel, the pool, a soft-play centre and a shopping mall. It was good for us to concentrate on trying to keep her amused and happy: we wanted to leave her with good memories to fall back on when we were no longer with her. But this was not the sunny Jessica we knew: she was quiet, and rarely smiled. She was good, she did as she was asked, she ate a little food and came along with us willingly enough to whatever we thought she'd like to do – but the spark had gone out of her. I noticed that she was wearing my little silver heart like a talisman, refusing to take it off for swimming or bath time. Each night she held tightly to my hand, still fearful of the dark, terrified to be alone. The more time I spent with her, the more forcefully it struck home that she was in desperate need of love, security and consistency. I wondered how much she had seen of her mother's affair, how many arguments she had witnessed between her parents, what she knew of those two men in jail. She made it clear she did not want to talk about what had happened, and we did not press her, feeling it would come out when she was ready. I was adamant about one thing though, we had to get her away for a while. I had the signed passport forms, and I took them to the British Embassy to get the passports.

It was not easy. I spent some time convincing an official at the embassy that Evelyn had given me permission to take the children for a holiday – he was clearly uncomfortable that she was not the one applying for passports and that I had filled out the forms myself. While the forms were being examined in one office, I was sent to see the immigration officer to ask about exit visas. He was even harder to persuade that the children's mother was agreeable to my taking them out of the country.

'Where is the mother of the children?' he barked. His tone made me nervous, and my pulse quickened.

'She is ill, and pregnant, and she cannot travel. But she has given me permission to apply for the visas. She will be joining us in the UK later this month.' My heart was hammering – I hoped I sounded calm and confident. He looked suspicious.

'I'm sorry, the mother or parent has to be present. The children are minors and these are the rules.' He turned away to shuffle papers. I wondered in a panic whether to tell him about Steven, about my suspicions about Evelyn, about the murder investigation. No, not yet. Keep it all above board.

'Please talk to the consul, he will explain,' was all I could think of saying. I was referring to Peter Hawkins. I felt he would be on our side.

He disappeared down a long corridor and was gone for what seemed like hours. On his return he said, 'You must go tomorrow at 8 am to Batayangalon City to the visa office. But I am sure they will want to talk to the mother of the children.'

That was something – an appointment at least. 'Thank you, there will be no problem,' I said, putting the visa forms into my bag. At that moment someone appeared with two small maroon books: the passports. I was halfway there.

That evening we played games with Jessica and then cuddled up on the bed with some story books. One of them had a picture of a child standing up in a cot, and on the other page an image of the child's parents in bed. Jessica looked at the page for a long time, and as I was tucking her up she said, 'Mummy doesn't love Daddy any more. She loves Arnold.' I went cold all over. 'Who is Arnold?' I asked, as if I didn't know. 'He sleeps in your kitty bed with Mummy.' She was referring to the bedroom Alan and I used to use: it had pink-and-white Hello Kitty curtains.

'Where is Daddy when Arnold sleeps with Mummy?' I asked gently.

'At the office. Mummy doesn't have clothes on, Nana. And Arnold kisses Mummy.'

Out of the mouths of babes, I thought. Jessica had seen way too much, and it had confused her. I knew she was telling me something that was important to her, something she did not understand, and was probably asking me to explain this complicated adult behaviour to her. I stroked her head – she was sleepy and I thought it best to change the subject. If she wanted to talk more about this I needed to be straight in my head about what I would say to her.

During the day, if I felt my grief welling up I would leave Jessica with Alan and slip into the bathroom to sit and weep silently. That night, I laid my head down on the pillow next to her sweet sleeping face and let the tears fall. Steven's ashes were in a white box by the side of the bed. I looked at her innocent face, which held such a look of Steven, and tried to accept the reality of his death. I felt so angry with Evelyn: this little girl should be with her dad, not with a couple of old fogeys.

The next day we made the hour-long journey to the visa office, only to find a long queue of other hopefuls snaking its way around the block. We were the only Western faces, and Jessica stayed close to us. After several hours we reached the window, and I handed over the letter from the consul together with the passports. Another official appeared, with some more forms for us to fill in and instructions to join another line. Again, we waited for ages before we eventually saw yet another official.

'Where is the mother?' he asked, predictably.

'She is at home with the other child. She is not well and she is pregnant. She is having a difficult time, Sir. Her husband – my son – was shot dead in a robbery. I want to help her.' He looked at me for some moments, and I held his gaze. He then beckoned us to follow him into another room.

Here we met a female officer, who sat down next to us and asked us what our intentions were. I repeated my story: I was trying to help my daughter-in-law by looking after her children while she recovered from a dreadful situation. She had a passport and visa and had asked me to get visas for the children.

'I'm sorry, the mother has to be present because the children are young and were born in the Philippines,' the officer said flatly, her face inscrutable.

'But the mother is not well,' I tried.

'Will the children be returning to the Philippines with the mother after the holiday?' asked the first official.

'Yes,' I said, feeling my hands go clammy. 'If she wants that for herself and the children. It is very difficult for her here, she has no family support.' This at least was mostly true.

They both disappeared with the forms, leaving us alone in the room. The air was stale and sticky. We sat in silence, hardly daring to talk in case they overheard us say something that would prejudice our case. Thankfully Jessica was playing quietly with some plastic figures. We watched her, and waited, and it felt like forever. Every time an official passed the door I would break into a sweat, panicking that we were in for more questioning, or would receive a blank 'Sorry, your application has been refused.' I knew I had stretched the truth rather excessively, but I hadn't hurt anyone. Yet here I was feeling like a criminal awaiting trial.

Eventually the woman officer returned, carrying some papers and the passports. 'I'm sorry for your loss,' she said. 'Take these papers to the cashier.' We held our breath, trying not to catch each other's eye. The cashier stamped the papers several times and asked us for fifteen hundred pesos, which we paid – and I'm sure my hands were trembling as I counted out the notes. He then handed us back the passports – and the visas. The precious visas.

Outside, we drank in the fresh, warm air and hurried for a

taxi, swinging Jessica along happily. She laughed, sensing our relief and excitement. We had done it – we had in our hands documents that gave us official permission to take our grandchildren to our home.

'All we have to do now,' I said to Alan that evening, 'is to get Evelyn's agreement for us to borrow the children for a while.'

'And enough evidence to have her arrested,' Alan replied. 'I've got a feeling that the police are so proud of themselves for catching two suspects they might think they have done enough.'

He was right: my grandmother's instincts were taking over and I was suddenly focussing on the children. I desperately wanted to take the kids home to the UK. But my duty as a mother was in conflict with this, and I knew we wouldn't be able to leave until we had enough evidence to prove beyond doubt that Evelyn was behind the murder of our son.

Events, however, were about to overtake us.

9
A Hasty Retreat

Jessica stayed with us for several days, still quiet and reluctant to eat much, but clearly loving the attention. Alan and I felt so happy spending time with her; we were enjoying teaching her things, reading to her, discovering together parts of the city we had not seen before. It cheered me up a little to feel that, in the midst of this great sorrow, we were finding occasional flashes of joy. I would catch myself laughing at something she did or said, and I would realise I hadn't thought of Steven for perhaps ten whole minutes. We were dreading the day she would have to go back to her mother, because who knew when we would get a chance to be with her again?

In the event, Evelyn failed to turn up in Makati on the morning we had agreed. We were waiting in the bus station, Jessie brushed and dressed and wearing a little backpack with her possessions in. 'I want to stay with you, Nana,' she kept saying. I choked back my tears and reassured her that we'd be seeing her again very soon. Perhaps Evelyn really was ill, as the police had reported. If so, why hadn't she called? So we decided to go off and enjoy our day. Evelyn could always contact us if she turned up. There was no call.

'Why didn't Mummy be here?' an anxious Jessie asked us later that night. 'Didn't she want Jessie?' I always believed, and still do, that no matter what you feel about a child's parent, it is not your place to plant negative ideas in their mind. I gave her a plausible explanation, told her that her mummy loved her very much and would come to get her when she could. 'I want Joshua,' Jessica said tearfully later that day. I could only guess at the turmoil she was feeling, and the only thing I knew – the thing I could do best – was to hug her and reassure her, and try to make her feel loved.

The next morning we had a call from Jose, our informant. He told us that Evelyn had been to visit Adoray in jail and, astonishingly, had given him a mobile phone. I could not believe the authorities would allow this, nor that it would not ring alarm bells for them. He also said that Joshua had been sent to a village in Daram Samar province, some thousand miles away, to stay with her relatives. Daram Samar – known as the 'pits of the Philippines' – the place where nobody ever wants to go or ever wants to be known to come from. There is absolutely nothing there. It was where Evelyn was born.

This was awful news – not only would it be impossible to get hold of Joshua, but also if this meant that Evelyn wasn't prepared to look after her baby, perhaps the same fate awaited Jessica. I could imagine her finding children a burden if her lover was languishing in jail, needing her help. Poor Joshua – what on earth would happen to him in Daram Samar? It was where Evelyn's family lived, and we had been there some years earlier – never again, I had vowed at the time. There was no running water, no electricity, very little food apart from fish, rice, coconuts and mangoes. Everybody lives, sleeps and eats in one room. This would come as a shock to little Joshua, who had had something of a Western upbringing already. He was used to milk, a balanced diet of soft but solid foods, and he needed comfort and familiarity. Alan and I spent hours discussing what we should do. Should we take the matter up with the embassy? Should we ask Evelyn to get him sent back so we could help look after him? Should we ask Jose to send someone to check up on the baby? Should we travel to the island ourselves to rescue him? I felt that we were rapidly getting out of our depth.

Some days later Evelyn called my mobile phone.

'I come today to collect Jessica.'

Oh no you don't, I thought. I'm not ready for her to be sent to the provinces. 'I'm sorry, Evelyn,' I said, thinking quickly. 'We're not in Makati, we are having a short holiday in Bagio.' This was a lush green mountain resort a few hours' drive from Manila, where we had been once with Steven. This was a lie, of course, but she had no way of knowing.

She hit the roof. Her already pidgin English descended into incomprehensible ranting, and I was silent until she finished.

'We waited for you, Evelyn, on the day we agreed. Where have you been?' I felt calm.

'I was there, I waited.'

Liar. 'When? Why didn't you call?'

'I was ill. I had a miscarriage.'

'I would have come to you, I could have helped,' I said, digesting this latest news and wondering what really happened.

'My family are taking care of me.'

'I would like to see your family – shall we come to Angeles to meet them?'

'They have left. And now I need money for a new house. Why you not give me money?' She was angry now.

'Don't worry. We will meet and talk about money. I would like to see Joshua too – how is he?'

'He is fine, Ma'am.'

'Good. We will call you from Makati on Friday when we return.' This gave me a few days' grace.

On top of the worry about the children, the police did not have happy news to report.

'You should leave, Madam,' said Reynoldo the next time we visited Makati police for an update. 'The family of

Dagami is very angry that you accuse him, and I worry you may not be safe. You are the person who will make the complaint about these two men, you will need to be at their trial, but if you are killed you cannot do this, and they could go free.'

My God. It made sense. I could see it would be more convenient for the accused men if we were out of the equation. If they had us bumped off, they would go free as there would be no one to push them to a trial, no one to make the 'complaint'. We had already heard that Martin had gone into hiding. I was too shocked to reply. Alan spoke for me: 'You think our lives are in danger?'

'I think it very likely.'

'We are already under 24-hour armed guard at our hotel. Isn't that enough?'

'Maybe not.'

I was scared now, and could see that the police were taking this seriously – I reckoned they knew more than they were letting on. Logic kicked in: if we had to think about leaving I would need all the documents, so I arranged to have the police files photocopied. While this was being done I asked one more time whether they could question Evelyn. More than that, feeling this could be my last chance, I begged, I pleaded with the man.

'I understand your wish, Madam, but we have no evidence. We have two prime suspects, please be happy with this.'

'Someone made them do it. Someone had a motive.' He nodded and shrugged. I wasn't getting anywhere, so we left, hastening back to our hotel in a cab for fear we were being watched. We did not dare to leave our hotel room for the rest of the day.

Hard on the heels of this meeting was a call from the consulate summoning us to the embassy.

'Oh, God, it must be about the visas. Perhaps they will

withdraw them.' This was a real worry, and it was with quaking hearts that we arrived in Peter's office.

'I'm afraid to say I believe you ought to think about leaving the country,' he said, after the usual pleasantries.

'Why?' I asked, knowing what was coming.

'This is a rather delicate situation. I completely understand why you have wanted to become so intensely involved with your son's case, and I hope you know how sympathetic we at the embassy are for your plight. But I have to say that your activities have ruffled quite a few feathers: I have arranged a meeting with the ambassador and the immigration officer for later this morning. We need to have a rational discussion about the situation.'

'I'd like my lawyer to be there, if that is all right,' I said, and called Christian, who arrived fairly smartly.

It was an interesting, if depressing, meeting. The ambassador had clearly been contacted by Oscar Ramos, the officer in charge of the case.

'We have learnt that the two accused men used to be drug-squad police officers and are now working as security guards,' he began. 'They are also thought to be involved in dealing drugs. This means several things. First, the police are protective of people they regard as insiders. Secondly, the accused men know people who have access to licensed firearms, and thirdly – if they are involved in the drug underworld – they will almost certainly have been associating with some highly undesirable characters.

'They know what you are up to, they know you're digging for more information – and these are people who will stop at nothing to prevent you from doing so,' added the ambassador.

We were silent while we digested this information. Then Alan spoke up:

'The police were able to arrest these two men solely

because of our assistance in the case. We have paid for informants and surveillance that would simply not have happened without us. We are beginning to understand the "tit for tat" mentality here, but we feel strongly that Steven's wife is behind the killing. If we can stay here a little longer we are confident we will get enough information to have her arrested too.'

'And don't forget there is a third gunman still on the loose,' I said.

The immigration officer cut in here. 'I find it hard to believe that a Filipina wife would kill her husband. I also think the children should be with their mother, and I am not happy about the grandparents taking them out of this country.'

'How did you come by British passports for the children? This is very unusual,' commented my lawyer. Honestly, whose side was he on? Sometimes it felt to me as if he had a residual loyalty to his fellow countrymen. I looked at Alan and rolled my eyes.

'The children's mother gave me permission,' I explained steadily. Things were not going our way. Jessica had been with us throughout the meeting and now I pulled her to me protectively.

'I think it would be better for the Department of Social Welfare to become involved now. They will ensure that the children are safe.' This came from my lawyer.

I looked at Peter, silently appealing for his help, and he inclined his head slightly as if to acknowledge what I was trying to say to him. I had come to realise that he was our only friend. There was a lot he could not do because of 'protocol', but at least he did not stand in our way.

'It is my personal feeling that Margaret and Alan would be best to leave today with Jessica. She has a British passport and a visa, and these, her grandparents, merely wish to give her a holiday – she has, after all, been through a difficult time.' This was directed to his colleagues, and he then turned to us. 'If the mother is indeed implicated, as you suggest, then I am sure the police will uncover sufficient evidence. I will be informing our counterparts in London that I have advised the three of you to leave the Philippines immediately. If you do not take this advice we cannot be responsible for your safety.'

'But what about Joshua?' I cried. 'He has been sent to a God-forsaken province miles away. We have no way of knowing if he is safe or not!'

'We will look into the situation, it may be possible to find out where he is – we have contacts with the DSW who know what to do in these circumstances.'

'Alan – I can't leave without Joshua. You go with Jessica to Hong Kong and I'll meet you there,' I said.

'No, Marg. I'm not going without you. I can't leave you here if you might be in danger.' He was right. I looked at Jessica, who was regarding the grown-ups with frightened eyes. I couldn't bear to lose her now. The room fell quiet – everyone was waiting for my decision. Suddenly the fatigue of the past month and a half, the worry, grief and exhaustion caught up with me. I just wanted it all to be over. I closed my eyes. Given the opposition from the immigration officer and my own lawyer, I suddenly realised that the embassy people were offering us a solution. Not a complete solution, but at least it would help Jessica.

'Very well,' I said quietly. 'We'll leave.'

The British Embassy is swift to act in situations like these: we were whisked in a special car to the airport ticket office, where we bought tickets for the next flight from Manila to Heathrow. We then had an hour to pack, and Peter Hawkins waited for us in our hotel lobby. It was all happening so fast – my mind was a blur, and I could hardly focus as we rushed around our room collecting papers, electronic equipment, clothes and books. Jessica sat hugging her knees and watching us, a secret smile on her face. Her eyes had lit up when we told her she was coming to England with us. Later, at the airport, we had an official escort to take us through immigration, to wait with us in the BA lounge, and, finally, to see us on to the plane. This at least forestalled any difficult questions about our taking Jessica out of the country without her mother.

'They're not taking any chances,' commented Alan wryly. 'They can't wait to see the back of us.' As the plane taxied towards the runway and took off into the night sky, I sent a hurried text message to my daughters to let them know we were on our way home. Then I sank back in my seat. I thought back to our flight out to Manila two days after Steven's death: it seemed to me as if it had been months ago. It was in fact a mere six weeks, but so much had happened, I was having trouble processing it all. Time, grief and stress do strange things to you – I was only fifty-one but I felt I had aged several years. I'm not vain, but I was aware that I looked rough as a dog – my face was drawn, my eyes puffy with so much crying, I had not been eating or sleeping well, and I was more tired I think than I had ever been. No doubt I had acquired many more grey hairs. The visits to the police station, the efforts to gather information, the worry and the fear, and the complex game of chess I had been playing with Evelyn had all taken their toll.

I cursed myself for not having been able to gather enough evidence to convict Evelyn, and that the third gunman was somewhere still in hiding. It would be hard to do anything from the UK, but I would just have to find a way. There were things to be thankful for though: two killers in jail, Steven's ashes safely tucked in my hand luggage, passports for the children, and his precious daughter sitting next to me. She snuggled closer to me and whispered, 'Don't ever leave me, Nana,' before dropping off to sleep.

Yet as the plane climbed further into the sky I felt my soul was being wrenched in two. We were leaving baby Joshua behind to an uncertain fate. I could not get the image of the little boy out of my mind. I had been there at his birth, and I had even been allowed to name him. Such an honour it was, and I felt I had a special bond with him because of this. It was just after my mother had died of cancer, so I was more emotional than usual. Steven kept picking him up in the hospital and handing him to me, like a present. Evelyn had been fine with this, and even the midwife had commented that she wasn't that interested in the baby. All the more reason for me to worry now. Oh, where was he and how on earth was I to find a way through the deceit and lies to help him?

My wonderful son, Steve, aged 14.
He always loved the sea.

Steve was a sensible boy but he had a sense of adventure as well.
He was an army cadet for a while and enjoyed it hugely.

Joe, Steve's dad. Steve was such a source of comfort and support to me after Joe died.

Steve, aged nineteen, me, Lucy and Catherine. We were always a very close family.

Even when Steve move to Hong Kong to work I saw him often. He w so excited about being there and I was thrille for him.

Evelyn aged about 14 and growing up fast.

Evelyn is about 12 here, with her mother in their home in the provinces. She came from a very poor background.

By the time she was 13, Evelyn was dancing in bars like this one, in Angeles City.

This photo of Steve with two of Evelyn's sisters was taken when he went to visit her family for the first time. He told me he wanted to rescue her.

And rescue her he did. Steve and Evelyn married just 8 months after they met. It pains me to see how proud he looks here.

They look so much in love on the honeymoon . . .

I was thrilled to be asked to go along with them for part of their honeymoon trip. It is hard to remember just how wonderful things seemed then.

Steve was always happy on boats especially when he'd caught such fantastic fish!

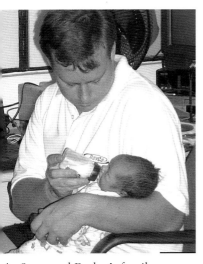

As Steve and Evelyn's family grew, so did the tensions and by the time Josh was born, Steve was under train. He loved being a dad though.

Evelyn was usually a pretty indifferent mother but this is a great photo of her and Jessica, on Jess's second birthday.

Steve was a committed family man but looking at this photo now, it seems obvious to me that the problems in his marriage were getting to him.

Throughout those years, I continued to visit. Alan and I even had plans to move to the Philippines.

This is the last photo of me and Steve together.
Six months later, he was dead.

My beloved son's coffin, in the chapel of rest.

rnold Adoray, Evelyn's lover and the first gunman.

Alex Dagami, the second gunman.

Evelyn approaching the courtroom on the first day of the trial.

I had to go to see for myself the jail where Evelyn, Adoray and Dagami would serve their time.

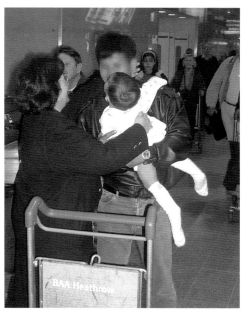

Finally, I had baby Josh safe in my arms, thanks to the wonderful work of Jose.

Four years since Steve's death and Jessica and Josh are now happy, healthy kids. Alan and I are determined to give them every bit of love.

10
Slow Progress

I was so pleased we were on a night flight, as the exhausted and bewildered Jessica slept most of the way. I looked down at her tenderly, wondering what she had seen in her short life, how much she really understood.

'I just hope we're doing the right thing,' I said quietly to Alan, who looked as pale and tired as I felt. Although we were ostensibly taking Jessica just for a holiday, I felt in my heart that this would be more than a few weeks.

'What alternative is there, Marg? If we left her here she'd be a bar girl by the age of twelve just like her mother. Either that or the rice fields. Evelyn didn't believe in education.' This was true, but my mind was a whirl of emotions: grief, guilt, regret, fear for the future – and sheer relief to be leaving that unforgiving country. I knocked back a couple of glasses of wine and soon fell asleep myself.

I awoke to find that we were circling Heathrow, and as the plane began its descent I reached into my hand luggage for a warm pair of trousers and a woolly for Jessica. The temperature had been up in the 80s in her country, but I knew that England at dawn on a late-summer morning would have a chill in the air. She wriggled and squirmed uncomfortably.

'It's itchy, Nana. I don't like it.' I realised with a jolt how much was about to change for her. She was used to wearing only pants and teeshirts, or thin sundresses at the most. Things like this hadn't occurred to us yet, and winter clothes were only the beginning. I tried to make it fun for her, a new adventure, but we'd have to take things slowly.

We were greeted at the airport by an emotional group of family members: my daughters, their families and my sisters. Everyone was laughing and crying at once – it was the first time we had all been together since Steven's death, and the first time that some of them had met Jessie. She was overwhelmed by all the strangers and gripped my hand even more tightly. Later that morning, the cab drew up outside our home, and we poured ourselves and our luggage onto the pavement. Alan busied himself with taking it up to our front door, and suddenly the enormity of what we were doing struck me. We were starting a new life, and I had to say something or the moment would pass and I might regret it for ever.

'Alan, hold on a minute,' I said, catching his arm. 'Look. When we married we agreed not to have children together. We had my three and that was enough. But look what we're about to take on here. If you have any doubts about the future, this new future where we are parents to Steve's children, now is the time to say.'

He looked at me, horrorstruck. 'What are you saying, Marg?'

'If we end up keeping Jessica, I need to be sure you are willing to do this job with me. As for me, I have no choice. You do. I won't love you any the less for it, but I have to ask you.'

He looked as though I had hit him.

'I loved Steven too, you know. I miss him as much as you do and we are going to do this together. I can't believe you would doubt that.' I felt crass and stupid then, sorry and guilty that I had even asked the question. Of course he wouldn't pull out now; what on earth was I thinking? I hugged him though my tears, and went to fetch the sleeping Jessica.

'You daft cow,' Alan muttered as he went towards the car.

There were flowers on the doorstep and as we opened the front door it pushed against a huge tide of post. Jessica walked in, wide-eyed. She had never seen a house like it, of course. It was decorated in a fashion unfamiliar to her, with carpets and warm furnishings unlike anything she had seen before. What was comfortable to us was alien to her. We had not been prepared for her, of course: we had no clothes, toys or even a spare bed. Over the next few weeks she was showered with hand-me-down clothes, a bike and a dolls' pram, and other gifts and toys from local friends. I had to keep much of it back for fear of confusing her – it would not be healthy to go from ordinary Filipina kid who was used to playing in the dirt in the squatters' compound to material Western girl overnight. She also needed to develop play skills she simply did not yet have, and this would take time and patience.

Gradually we opened the hundreds of messages of sympathy and condolence. There was considerable interest in our plight from the local press, and friends and neighbours and even strangers had contacted us with offers of help and, to our surprise, money. It was comforting to think that our case had touched so many, yet I found it hard to talk to these kind people and to accept their support. During these first few weeks back in England I was in a lonely dark place, contemplating the huge hole in my life, which – instead of becoming easier to cope with – seemed to become more unbearable each day. Being home, without the daily visits to Makati police station to give the day shape, and with the quietness and familiarity of my own house, it started to dawn on me that this was how the future looked. Months, years decades – all without Steven, stretching ahead interminably. This seemed unimaginable. He had been so much part of the fabric of my life: I used to check my computer each morning for a little box indicating that Steve was there to chat online. 'Hi Mum, Steve here,' it would say. Our year was structured around the times when we would spend long holidays with him. Not only was there a deep emotional gulf, but we were facing an entirely different future from the one we had fondly imagined for ourselves.

For, ironically, it was the very next month that we had been supposed to be moving to the Philippines for good. I had qualified some eight years earlier with a Masters degree in medical science. Initially I wanted to use this to add to my social science degree so that my work in residential care homes could broaden to take in the medical side – and in fact I had run my own units for adults with learning difficulties. However, as we learnt more about the poverty and deprivation in the Philippines, and laid our plans for moving out there, I decided I would be able to put my skills to good use where they were really needed. My first plan was to do a research project on the street children in Angeles, and then I planned to adopt some of the children. A children's centre there had already offered me a job as a counsellor and teacher. This had been a particular interest of Steven's: he had helped fund the building of the centre and had taken us to see orphanages and the impoverished areas of the city. 'There's so much work to be done, Mum,' he would sigh. 'It will be great to have you here, helping.' I'll never forget the orphanages he showed us – row after row of sad little children sitting in their cots, arms outstretched. I was determined that one day I would help them, and Steven convinced me that giving the children a bit of self-worth, helping them towards independence, teaching them to write their name – these little things could mean so much. So here were more lives that, indirectly, Steven's murderer had damaged.

Yet here I was, with one almost-orphan in my care, and another haunting my dreams.

I absorbed myself by day in helping Jessica settle in. She was very quiet at first, taking in her new world, sitting very still – often on the floor on her haunches, as was the custom in the Philippines – and looking around her with big wide eyes. If a stranger approached her she clung to me, and if the doorbell rang she would run to me in fear. The first time this happened I heard her whisper 'Is it Arnold?' – and the horrifying thought hit me that she had actually been afraid of her mother's lover. What had he said, what had he done to her? Had he threatened her, in order to ensure her silence? She was terrified of the dark, and as I gradually tried to wean her out of our bed and into her own, her fear increased. One night she explained:

'I think the Aswang will get me. Don't let the Aswang take me away.'

I looked this up in my book on folk culture, and I read: *Primitive peoples in the provinces tell their children stories to keep them safe and close to their mothers. One of these features the Aswang – a ghost that takes children away if they wander far from their village.* I imagined Evelyn passing these superstitions on to her child and felt angry and sad. Perhaps Evelyn herself had even believed in stories like this.

'The Aswang doesn't come to England. There are no Aswangs here. This is a safe place, Jessie. You don't need to worry, Nana and Papa are here, and we will always take care of you.'

As much as we tried to be gentle and keep the new experiences spread out, almost everything we took for granted was unusual to her. She had never seen a bath, only a shower. She had never used a toilet, always peeing in a potty or in the garden. And at every opportunity she would strip off all her clothes quite unselfconsciously, wandering around in only her panties. Food was another big issue, and she would only eat fruit at first, not being used to our basic meat-and-two-veg-type staple meals – although I tried (not very successfully) to replicate the noodles and fried chicken she loved. Every time she sat down to eat she would push her plate towards me and say, 'Save this for Joshua. He is hungry, Nana,' and I would have to take a little and make as if I was keeping it for her brother, and then she would smile and have something to eat herself. I prayed to God that he wasn't hungry, but I suspected she was right.

She thought about him all the time, I could see. In her room she was creating a little nest of toys and clothes for him that no one was allowed to touch. I was astounded at such a caring and compassionate instinct, and felt proud of my little granddaughter. I wondered if she had been forced to care for her brother when her mother was busy elsewhere.

'This is for my baby Joshua. He will come here and be happy. When will Joshua come to me, Nana? I think he is sad now.' And I would always reassure her that he would come soon. Sometimes she asked about Evelyn: 'Why Mama not here with Jessie?', to which I would reply that maybe she would get a ticket and come soon. It was impossible to know what to say to this little girl, but what I did say had to be consistent – that was clear. I knew I had a great responsibility not to warp her impressionable and developing mind with unhappy thoughts about her mother, but I was eaten up with anger at this woman who could put her own child in this situation. It was hard to hide my feelings all the time, and sometimes she would catch me with tears pouring down my face.

'Why you cry, Nana?'

'Because I miss your daddy.'

'I miss my daddy. My mummy is bad, she eat all the food and me and Joshua have nothing. Daddy buy me food.' I knew Steven did much of the caring and shopping, but it shocked me that Jessica was so aware of the disparity between him and Evelyn. I decided it was important to talk about her life in the Philippines, and to talk about Steven so she would not lose the memories she did have. We would sit together, cuddling and crying at times, but I tried to remember funny stories to make her laugh: 'Do you remember the time Daddy pretended to eat the hamster on toast?' 'Do you remember how you used to jump on my bed in Daddy's house and take my lipstick and run away with it?' I showed her photographs and she stuck some up on her bedroom wall. These developed into a display of all the people she cared most about, so I bought a big sheet of paper and headed it 'Jessica's Family'. We included photos of her Filipino grandparents, cousins, aunts and uncles, as well as everyone she was starting to meet in England. It proved to be very helpful to her understanding of the different people we talked about, and her place in the world. Of course I included a large and beautiful picture of her mother.

I wondered what to do about Evelyn. As far as I knew, she had no idea we had left the Philippines, and she would no doubt be contacting me any day now to arrange collection of Jessica. I felt guilty, and sorry that she would be without her daughter for some time, but also secure in the knowledge that what I had done had been with the full support of the British Embassy. We had left in such a rush that day that I had not been able to contact Jose and Juliana and let them know what we were doing. So while my days were taken up with Jessica, at night I sought refuge in my computer, firing off emails to my MP, my UK lawyer, my Filipino lawyer, the British Embassy in Manila, and anyone else I could think of who might be able to put pressure on the police to pursue their investigation against Evelyn and the third gunman. I knew deep down that Evelyn had organised the murder, but still I prayed with all my heart that she was innocent. If only they could just get her in for questioning, then at least we'd know something more.

I should not have worried about Jose and Juliana: it was after all their business to ferret out information, and after a couple of days I started to receive emails from Juliana.

> To: Margaret Davis
> From: Juliana Abucay
> Date: 27 August 2002
>
> Hello Tita Margaret
> I hear from people that you are in the UK. Is all everything OK? I still try to find out about Evelyn, she is moving house today and Joshua is in Vasayer. Mama Rosario has bad foot and needs medicine, please Tita can you send money.
> Waiting to hear.
> Juliana

Tita was an affectionate name, meaning 'auntie'. Mama Rosario was Evelyn's aunt who had already helped us with the statement. I reckoned she would still be able to help us, and I was happy to send money if she was sick – but before I did I hoped I could persuade her to find more information: I had already learnt that money was a great motivator, although I wasn't sure how to send money to a person in another country. Vasayer was the name of a remote village in the province of Daram Samar. I stalled, asking Juliana for more news on Evelyn's plans, and whether her sister Carmen – the wife of the third gunman who had been positively identified by Martin's girlfriend – had said anything. According to Rosario, she definitely knew something. I needed them to try to get hold of Joshua, but I wasn't yet sure how to do this. If conditions were rough for children on the streets of Manila, they were worse in the provinces, and I doubted his immune system was up to coping with the infections he'd be exposed to. Steven knew this too – he never allowed Evelyn to take the children to the provinces.

To: Margaret Davis
From: Juliana Abucay
Date: 29 August 2002

Thank you Tita Margaret for promising money. When I saw Joshua with Evelyn, I tell to myself poor Joshua you got a wrong mother, don't worry your grandmother do everything for good future for you. I don't know about Carmen's husband, nobody know where he is, but I must help Mama Rosario she is not well and God helped her tell the truth about Evelyn and Arnold, I tell her not to worry you not forget promises.
Take care
Juliana

Ah, so the third gunman was in hiding. If only I could find some way of getting him to talk – he must know what happened that night. Could his wife persuade him?

To: Juliana Abucay
From: Margaret Davis
Date: 30 August 2002

Alan is finding out from Western Union today how to mail money to you. Carmen is not in a good position with her husband on the run. If he knows something and will talk to the police maybe I can help get a better deal for him. Can you ask Carmen to talk to Evelyn about Joshua coming to me? I must know what Evelyn is planning for Joshua, I am worried. Can you ask someone to speak to her and ask if he can come to me? Tell Mama Rosario I have not forgotten the brave thing she did for me.
Speak soon
Your friend Margaret

We hadn't been home above a fortnight when I had a call on my mobile phone from Evelyn. I was expecting it but it still took me unawares, and my heart leapt into my mouth. I had to be careful what to say. She did not know that I was in England, and I was polite and friendly, agreeing to meet her a few days later and return Jessica to her. I asked her to bring Joshua with her. 'No, Ma'am, he is teething,' she lied. I decided to play her at her own game.

'Then I think it is best to bring Jessica to you when Joshua is well enough to see me.' Perhaps this would encourage her to go and get her baby. She shouted something at me and the line went dead. I then called Juliana to ask her if there was any news.

'Ma'am, Evelyn's family are mad at her for what happen to Steven. I think I can get Joshua but they want money for him.'

'They can have money, that's fine. How much do they want?'

'200,000 peso.' So this was what a child's life was worth to them. A couple of thousand pounds. Were they prepared to sell their grandson to me without telling their daughter? I wondered how much they knew about Evelyn's involvement in the killing.

'OK, Juliana. This is what we'll do. I will send the money to Mama Rosario and she will be responsible for dividing it amongst the people who help us to get Joshua.'

'There is another problem, Tita Margaret. Joshua is sick.'

'How sick?' My heart started hammering. What a mother, to abandon her child to this place. I had heard of children dying from malaria and other tropical diseases on these islands.

'I don't know – he has sores, he has lost weight, he cries all the time. I take him to doctor when I get him, maybe give him milk and food and medicine.'

Oh Jesus. I thought about the sick children I'd seen there and feared the worst. I was gripped by a sense of urgency and had to convey this to Juliana. 'The sooner I have him at home with Jessica the better. Do you understand how important this is?'

'Yes, we will do our best. I'm happy Jessie is with you, she would have a bad life here with Evelyn and be working in the bars when she is very young.'

'OK, Juliana. Please tell me also if there is any news on Carmen and Roberto. Our lawyer can do a deal for him if he gives himself up. Steven liked him, I do not think he is a bad man: maybe he did not realise what the others were going to do.'

'He is hiding in the provinces; he is scared the associates of Arnold Adoray will kill him. I will try to get the message to him. Also Rosario offer to Evelyn she can live with her.'

This was mixed news. If Evelyn went to stay with Rosario I would be able to keep tabs on her, which was good. The danger was that she might get wind of what my informants and I were up to.

Meanwhile I had heard nothing from the embassy, although I had left many messages asking if a demand to go in for questioning – a subpoena – had been served on Evelyn. No news either from my Filipino lawyer; just a colossal bill. I looked at it in shock – it was to cover arranging the cremation (which Steve's colleagues actually did); negotiating with Evelyn for the children and Steve's ashes (which they failed at), and for following up police progress on Evelyn's case. Just because I was a Westerner they assumed I had money to burn. In fact all this was bankrupting me, and Alan and I were taking steps to remortgage our home.

I tried my county councillor contact again – he was already aware of my case, as I had kept him up to date from the Philippines. I counted him as something of a friend, as when he was standing as a local councillor I had been a member of the selection committee that appointed him and I had helped him campaign. However, when I called him he was less than helpful. Since the days knocking on the doors up and down streets near where I lived, I was now living in a different part of Nottingham. 'Try the North Notts MP, Margaret. I can't help you,' was his dismissive response. I can't deny I felt bitter about this. 'Typical,' I raged to Alan after this rebuff. 'He was all sweetness and light when I was his little runabout, but now I'm in trouble he doesn't want to know.' So I wrote to my MP – Ken Clarke. I waited for a reply, but all I got was a standard postcard acknowledging receipt of my letter. I was angry, but I was learning not to expect much from officialdom. *If you want to get anything done*, my old mum used to say, *do it yourself*. I was rapidly finding out the truth of her words.

A few days later Juliana called me in tears. She told me that she had received threatening text messages on her mobile phone. One read, '*What you did is a big problem. You don't know that I know you*,' and the other, '*Be careful, I know what you are doing*.' Poor Juliana was terrified. She had four children, the youngest of whom was only three, and she now feared for their lives. This was the work of Evelyn, I was sure of it. She was now living with Rosario, so it was possible she had overheard them talking.

To: Margaret Davis
From: Juliana Abucay
Date: 5 September 2002

Hello Margaret
Evelyn is so tanga [stupid], she has pawned her aunt's television, and Rosario very mad at her. But Rosario think Evelyn plans to get Joshua from Vasayer, I hope Rosario can persuade Evelyn to let

Joshua live with her, Rosario. I have to ask you, my husband Jose
– he ask is there chance for work in the UK and can you give us
supporting papers? The job situation is not good here. Your
friend, Juliana

This was good work – if Joshua could be got to Rosario he
would be accessible to us. Alan and I discussed their proposal
for coming to the UK, and we thought it only fair to help
them in exchange for the help they were giving us. I told
Juliana he would need to get a passport and a holiday visa.
We would be able to sign papers for them, but they were to
tell no one of their plans. In the back of my mind I was
developing a plan: if Joshua was eventually found, someone
would need to bring him to England. Jose could well be that
person.

Later that week I had a letter from Evelyn's lawyer that filled
me with dread. She was filing a case against me for kidnapping Jessica.

'Alan,' I reported grimly, 'we're in deep trouble.' He read
the letter.

'This is ridiculous, and you know it. She's just trying it
on.' I did know this, of course, but I couldn't get rid of the
gnawing sense of fear and guilt. Every time I thought of the
word 'kidnap' my stomach did a somersault.

I explained in a letter to this lawyer, as clearly as I could,
that I had not kidnapped the child but that Evelyn had left
her with me for ten days and had not been in contact. I was
concerned for her son in the provinces as Evelyn had no
money to support him, but I was more than willing to bring
Jessica back as soon as I was sure she had a home for her.
Alan and I were merely caretaking the children, temporarily
giving them a safe place. I also made the point that Steven's
estate was still tied up in probate and I was trying to protect

Evelyn and her children's financial interests by organising for his share of the business to be put into trust for the children, and for Evelyn. Privately, of course, I hoped she would be in jail before getting her hands on any of Steven's money. This was the loot he had been murdered for.

Martin called with some good news: he had been in to the police station to identify the two suspects formally. The line was bad as we spoke, but I did take on board that the prosecution lawyer had asked several leading questions about Evelyn. I also heard that the court had been given the evidence that Steven and Evelyn had not been on good terms at the time of the murder; that Evelyn had been having a relationship with Arnold Adoray; that there was no forced entry on the night of the murder; and finally that she had behaved oddly on the morning after the murder. I hoped this would lead to another arrest, and my lawyer told me the subpoena summoning her for questioning was ready to be served.

To: Margaret Davis
From: Juliana Abucay
Date: 13 September 2002

Evelyn has no money to travel to get Josh, so Rosario angry with her and ask me for money from you and she will go herself. The mother of Evelyn is angry also, it would be good to have some money for her too. Tell me what you think. Evelyn has not met me before and today I spoke to her, I ask if she has kids and we talk, and she tell me that she cross with Steve's mum for taking his things and she can get many money from her children because of their dad.
See, I get you good information
Juliana.

This was a bit garbled, but it was clear that Evelyn regarded the children as bargaining chips, as a means to an end for her.

I couldn't believe she wasn't going to get Joshua herself; she must know he wasn't well. Surely her arrest must be imminent? All we were waiting for was for Reynoldo Hernandez – the officer in charge – to get round to serving the subpoena. I told Juliana I thought we should wait until then to get Joshua, in order to avoid a fight with Evelyn. But the days slipped by, I spoke to Christian daily, and still Evelyn was not approached by the police. I was tearing my hair out in frustration: if only I could be there to put pressure on them.

To: Margaret Davis
From: Juliana Abucay
Date: 17 September 2002

Tita, Joshua is ill he has a rash on his body and he is bleeding, he has lost weight. The family cannot keep him and talk of giving him to child services. Tell me what you decide. Hoping to hear, Juliana

Oh my God. In desperation I called the consul in Manila to ask if I should just turn up and get him. I was prepared to travel the thousand miles to the provinces. I was prepared to take any amount of money with me. Peter Hawkins at the embassy was wary of giving me permission to do this, as the two accused men were receiving their bail hearing the next day: if they were released it could be very dangerous for me. What about sending someone from the Department of Social Welfare to get him? This was possible, but it would mean that Joshua would go into care until a court decided his fate – and I was well aware of how long that might take. Was it best for him, though, if he was suffering? Furthermore, I was shocked to hear that if I arrived in the Philippines with a case filed against me for kidnapping I could be arrested. Kidnapping carries an automatic death sentence in the Philippines. 'I'm prepared to take that risk, Peter,' I said stoutly. He persuaded me to wait a day and then decide. I put the receiver down. I knew I had to take matters into my own hands – get Joshua to a safe place and somehow pick him up myself. This was a matter of life and death: I would not be able to live with myself if anything happened to that little boy. Neither could I bear the thought of him languishing in an orphanage for months. I had seen these orphanages with my own eyes, and I was not about to condemn Joshua to months of state-sponsored neglect.

The next thing, then, was to find out exactly where Joshua was.

To: Juliana Abucay
From: Margaret Davis
Date: 17 September 2002

Where exactly are Evelyn's parents in Samar? Do you have the address? Who can get him to Angeles the soonest?
In haste, Margaret

To: Margaret Davis
From: Juliana Abucay
Date: 18 September 2002

I don't know exact address, there are no roads and streets, but Rosario can find her family and she will go to Samar to get Joshua if you send money now, money also for Evelyn mother. She is eldest sister and it is Philippine tradition for eldest sister to be in charge of family matters. She tells Evelyn to go to Bataan to stay with other family, she not want Evelyn in house no more Evelyn not pay her. Jose will get Joshua from Rosario in Angeles and take him to doctor, then you tell us what to do. We wait your decision. Juliana.

Bataan was a neighbouring province that was slightly easier to get to, and it was where another branch of Evelyn's family lived. I let Peter know what I was organising, and with his approval I wired some money immediately to Juliana. But I was worried about the elderly lady with the bad feet travelling such a long way by herself, so I asked Jose to go with her. And I didn't want Evelyn's mother to have any money until Joshua was safely back home with me. On the other hand, would Rosario be able to persuade her to hand the child over unless she could swap him for cash? I had an image in my mind of Joshua covered in sores, crying and frightened. How could his mother not be with her sick child? It beggared belief. Meanwhile, why had she still not been questioned by the police? I asked Peter to do everything he could to look into this.

To: Margaret Davis
From: Peter Hawkins
Date: 19 September 2002

Dear Margaret
I am going to the City Hall in person now to find out what the hold-up is. Your lawyer says he cannot understand the delay. The court is keen for Evelyn to explain herself and is asking why CID has not brought her in. Dagami and Adoray have not been granted bail but still I would be happy to conclude matters without your personal return here.
I will keep you informed.
Best wishes
Peter

To: Margaret Davis
From: Juliana Abucay
Date: 20 September 2002

Rosario not happy to get Joshua if no money for Evelyn mother. I see Evelyn and she tell me you meet her on Thursday in Makati.

Can you explain me what next?
Juliana

To: Juliana Abucay
From: Margaret Davis
Date: 20 September 2002

You must tell Rosario I keep my promises. Evelyn's mother will get money when Joshua is safe with me. Do not believe Evelyn, she is a dangerous, desperate, lying person. She has not been in contact with me.
Your friend
Margaret

This was getting tricky. I felt as if I was trying to control a game of Chinese whispers, without much success. Later that day I heard from Peter that the delay on the subpoena had been due to problems formatting a document. I laughed hollowly: the incompetence of this police force would have been funny if it wasn't so tragic. He assured me that it was currently being looked at by a police lawyer and would be served the next week. I wasn't convinced – that police officer Reynoldo was a ditherer who needed a bomb behind him. I'm not a conspiracy theorist by nature, but I was starting to wonder if he was afraid of the case coming to court because the two suspects were ex-police with friends who had access to guns. If they had only done their job properly from the beginning, all four culprits would be in jail and the children would be living a healthy and happy life with me and Alan in the UK. Because of their failures and delays my grandson was now in grave danger.

I also heard from my lawyer, who had been in court for the second bail hearing at which Reynoldo Hernandez was cross-examined, as was another police officer who was present at the original arrest of the two suspects. Adoray's lawyer failed to turn up, and bail was refused. Then I received this from Steve's friend:

To: Margaret Davis
From: Martin Beck
Date: 21 September 2002

Hi Margaret, bad news from me I'm afraid. I'm getting death threats now because I am a witness. I've decided to leave the PI, can't say where I'm going but will keep in touch via email. Martin.

Hmm. It sounded as if Evelyn and her nasty friends were getting desperate as the trial date approached. This was witness intimidation, pure and simple.

To: Margaret Davis
From: Juliana Abucay
Date: 21 September 2002

Evelyn say she go to get Joshua herself as she has meeting with you next week, she will exchange Joshua for Jessie and you will give her money, she says. We not tell her our plans, Jose ready go to tomorrow. But must have money for Evelyn mother. J.

So they were going to pre-empt Evelyn and snatch Joshua before she got to him. I turned this over and over in my mind – should I send money into the void before I knew he was safe? Could I really trust Evelyn's mother? She ought to have Joshua's best interests at heart, but she might have her own views as to what these were. I had liked the old lady when I had met her soon after the wedding, but what if she was as motivated by money as I suspected her daughter was? In all conscience I could not hand over money before I had little Joshua safe and sound. So, with a heavy heart, I gambled.

To: Juliana Abucay
From: Margaret Davis
Date: 22 September 2002

If Rosario cannot do this for me and cannot persuade her sister to take a sick child to get medical help then I will come myself to fetch Joshua. Or tell them to keep Joshua if they want. None of you will get anything.

It worked.

To: Margaret Davis
From: Juliana Abucay
Date: 23 September 2002

OK Rosario talk to Evelyn sister Carmen. She ready to go take Joshua to family in Bataan. That part of family very angry with Evelyn and happy to give Joshua to you, they want to help him.
Juliana

This was a huge relief, and I waited impatiently for news that the baby had been collected and was on the way to Bataan. But, day after day each message from Juliana brought no news about him, and she seemed concerned that perhaps Josh had been too ill to travel. Perhaps it really was time to bring the social services in – at least they would give him medical help. Or maybe it was just that Carmen was taking the journey slowly? Perhaps she was getting medical attention for him? It was a long way, of course. Over a thousand miles across bumpy roads in rickety buses, and the final part of the journey by boat. I was out of my mind with worry, and tried to busy myself with chasing up my lawyer and making preparations for Jessica's fourth birthday.

Then things started to move on another front:

To: Margaret Davis
From: Juliana Abucay
Date: 29 September 2002

Hello Tita, I talk to a girl called Aurora, she was maid to Evelyn and knows about Arnold, I think she has good information for police – she says she knows Evelyn want kill Steven. She needs a mobile phone, can you get one for her? Then I think she will speak, she is good person. Evelyn has job working in bar but not much money because her body is of a woman who has kids. And she not happy, she like a rag with nothing. She sell all things in house, even children beds and toys.
Yours, Juliana.

'Have a look at this, Alan,' I said, walking over to him with a printout of this email in my hand. 'She's clearly not expecting to have the children back, then. Not even Joshua.'

'My God – selling their toys. And she's back in the bars, I see.'

'Remember what that American guy said: "You can take the girl out of the bar but you can't take the bar out of the girl." She's reverting to type.'

'It's what she knows she can do, I expect,' said Alan, his sympathetic impulses aroused. 'Do you remember her telling us that in the provinces families are so large that children are lucky if they get fed, and girls' first sexual encounters are often with their father around the age of eleven? Coming from such a background, it's hardly surprising she has gone back to the only way of making money she has ever known.'

'Apart from marrying a Westerner,' I cut in. I could accept the dehumanising influence Evelyn's childhood experiences might have had on her, and that in marrying Steven she had been exposed to a world of luxury beyond her wildest imaginings – but I wasn't in the mood to try to understand. Nothing, but nothing, excused murder.

I was glad to hear about the maid who would talk, but every time I heard more evidence against Evelyn, or Evil-Lyn as I was now calling her to myself, I felt sickened to my very soul. How could she have taken that oath of innocence over Steven's dead body? She swore on the life of her mother and children she had nothing to do with his murder. Still, I felt this was good progress – the net was closing in on her now, with more people prepared to give information. Juliana had told me of another girl called Maria who was also ready to talk. Perhaps the tide was turning, and the consciences of those who knew the truth were being pricked. I readily agreed to giving them both gifts if they would call my lawyer and make a statement, but I always insisted that the money was for their bravery in telling the truth, and emphasised constantly that this was a quest for justice that they were helping with. Cynical friends and neighbours at home accused me of bribing people for information, believing that these people were so poor they would say anything for money. I didn't believe this was true, particularly because Filipino families tend to close ranks and protect their own in situations like this. I had to retain some faith in human nature to get me through these months of waiting and hoping.

But honestly, how much more evidence did we need to connect Evelyn with the murder? I had to keep everyone motivated until we could piece all the bits of the puzzle together, and then hope that the police would do their job. I felt like a puppet-master pulling strings, but these were puppets that had a life of their own.

11
Reunion

September 27 was Jessica's fourth birthday. The first birthday without her daddy, was all I could think. She rushed
downstairs that morning to find balloons on her chair and a
small array of presents around her breakfast bowl. I was
desperate to make this a special day for her. 'Shall we watch
the video of your third birthday?' I asked her, after she had
opened her presents. 'You'll see Mummy and Daddy.' We
had a whole shelf of videos sent to us over the years by Steve,
all labelled neatly.

And there, suddenly, was the little family, in the popular
burger chain Jolleebee. The footage was a bit shaky but you
could hear excited chatter and laughter and see everyone.
Evelyn looked beautiful, holding a three-month-old Joshua
in her arms. Jessica was running around wildly. And there
was Steve, my Steve, smiling from ear to ear and holding her
on his knees while she blew out the candles on her huge pink
cake. I thought it would be nice for her to see her family on
her birthday, and remember happy times, but it was a big
mistake. She looked up at me with tears welling in her eyes.
'Where are my mummy and daddy? Where is my baby
Joshua?'

'Daddy is in Heaven, sweetie. Joshua will come soon.'
And Mummy, I didn't say, might call you later if you're
lucky. I distracted Jessica by getting her ready to go out: I
had organised a day for the family at a little theme park
near our home that catered for the under-tens. We had a
lovely time, and I was so pleased that everyone was there

to give Jessica a normal birthday with fun and laughter.
But when we cut the cake and sang Happy Birthday I
faded into the background, sick with the pain of missing
Steven, and gnawed by pity for this little girl who was
growing up with the wrong people. I felt guilty for being
sad, yet even guiltier when I was happy. I laid my head
against the cool wall and allowed the sounds of the party
to wash over me. In the midst of the din I heard a small
voice:

'Can I save a piece of cake for my brother? He will come
soon.'

Evelyn did not call to wish her daughter a happy birthday.
She sent no card. No email. I wondered what could be going
through her mind on this day of all days.

> To: Margaret Davis
> From: Juliana Abucay
> Date: 29 September 2002
>
> Hello Tita, no news on Joshua but something funny from Aurora.
> She says Arnold has tattoo on his butt that says 'Evelyn I love
> you'. Also Maria has got a book with letters from Arnold to Evelyn,
> very good information, we give to lawyers. I hear also that Arnold
> wife Liezl go to Evelyn and ask money, but Evelyn don't have
> money anymore.
> I trust in God for Joshua, I hope news soon.
> Juliana

Here was yet more evidence against Evelyn, but the strain
of waiting and worrying was becoming too much for me. I
just wanted Joshua, and almost felt that I'd give up on the
pursuit of Evelyn if only I could rescue the little boy. It was
a week since Carmen had left to look for him, and after I'd
had a long talk with Alan we decided to ask the DSW to go
to find him. Joshua's safety had to be the most important

thing: they had faster means of travel at their disposal and could be there in a few hours. They soon reported back, however. Joshua was nowhere to be found in Daram Samar. I did not know whether to fear the worst, or hope that somehow Carmen had him safe. I had to keep hoping, if only for little Jessie's sake. Every morning she would wake full of excitement and ask me, 'Will baby Joshua come today, Nana?' and every morning I would reply, 'Not today my love. Soon, I hope.'

To: Margaret Davis
From: Juliana Abucay
Date: 2 October 2002

I now so worry I ask nephew of Mama Rosario to go to Vasayer. Many children die in Vasayer from infection. He teenager but strong and sensible, and if Joshua still in Vasayer he call Mama Rosario and she go to fetch Joshua.
Take care
Juliana

To: Margaret Davis
From: Juliana Abucay
Date: 3 October 2002

No news yet, Carmen not yet arrive in Vasayer, it takes 24 hours. Something else now, we have a plan for getting Palabay to talk. Jose talk to nephew of Rosario, name Mario Villamar. He say if Palabay confess what he know then he will be safe, you will help him. If yes, then Mario go find Palabay and tell him this. If you say yes I call your lawyer to arrange. Waiting to hear. JA.

To: Juliana Abucay
From: Margaret Davis
Date: 4 October 2002

Yes, that is a good idea to ask Mario to be a go-between. Are you sure
he is trustworthy? If so I will tell my lawyer to draw up a document
with the police. Can you find Evelyn and ask her where Joshua is?
Please Juliana it is VERY important, I cannot wait much longer, it is
making me ill not knowing. We are sending your money, around 5pm
your time tomorrow. I will never forget what you are doing for us.
Your friend
Margaret

To: Margaret Davis
From: Juliana Abucay
Date: 4 October 2002

Good news at last. Mario talked to the village elder who say that
Joshua still in Vasayer, not so ill but very thin, he not used to hard
living. I think best to get him to Manila to parents of Jose, but
please send money for milk. Aurora has talked to police, and
showed them letters from Arnold to Evelyn. One I wrote down, it
says 'Dear Honey, it's very hard for me to stay in jail I miss you so
much. I love you no one can separate us, I want to be free so that
we can see each other again. Love Ado.'
God has helped us, this is good information.
Juliana

Quickly I replied, saying yes get Rosario's son to take Joshua
to Jose's parents in Manila at once. I was so relieved I
grabbed Jessica and swept her along to the park, laughing
madly. She looked bewildered – I don't think she could
remember ever having seen me this happy. 'Joshua will be
here soon,' I shouted into the windy autumn afternoon as I
pushed her on the swings. She echoed me in a sing-song
voice: 'Joshua will be here soon, Joshua will be here soon.'

That night I fired off more emails: to the police, to my lawyers, and more money to the informants. Keeping all the balls up in the air was making me dizzy, but I had to keep going: I felt we were very close. I prayed that Mario would be able to persuade Carmen's husband to talk. He was, after all, a family member, and I suspected that by now Evelyn's family just wanted to settle all this fuss and go back to their quiet simple lives. Her sister must be out of her mind with worry, and it was probably she who was best placed to persuade her husband to give himself up.

To: Margaret Davis
From: Juliana Abucay
Date: 6 October 2002

Tita – Evelyn hear of our plan to get Joshua for you, and she say Joshua will see Steven before he see his grandmother. This sounds bad but I think she scared, I don't think she really do bad thing to Joshua. Evelyn parents not happy to give Joshua to Rosario nephew, he too young. I talk to Mario he may be better.

When I read that, I was more determined than ever to see Evelyn behind bars. How dare she make threats like this? Over the next few days the maid Aurora gave her statement to the police, Mario collected a letter from my lawyer to show to Palabay promising that he would be offered protection for a confession, and I continued to drip-feed them money. Joshua remained in Vasayer, but at least he was being given milk and food – according to Rosario's nephew – and would soon be ready for the journey. It was a real blow that Evelyn's family would not relinquish him to the nephew, but I was hopeful that Mario would help persuade them. I could hardly stay away from my Microsoft Outlook in box, obsessively checking it every half hour in case news came in. And finally it did.

To: Margaret Davis
From: Juliana Abucay
Date: 11 October 2002

Dear Tita Margaret

Good news. Mario convince Evelyn parents to give you Joshua – of course with a gift from you. They need 50,000 peso and they want to bring him to Manila themselves. This money also for air condition hire car because Joshua has many infection and rashes. Please send money fast in case Evelyn parents change minds. You must trust to Mario, he good man, I'm sure we can get Joshua. It is 3am here I'm sleepy please send word.

Your friend, Juliana.

'Alan!' I cried upon reading this. 'They've agreed! Evelyn's parents will hand him over.'

Alan rushed up the stairs and threw his arms around me, and read the email again and again, and we both stood crying with relief and happiness. 'We're not there yet, though, let's not get too excited, Marg. They may change their minds.'

'I've just got to wire the money, I really feel we're there. I'm so happy! I think her parents are genuine people, they must be shocked at what Evelyn has done.'

'I just hope Evelyn doesn't get wind of this and try to spoil it. She knows some right dodgy types, believe you me. It could get dangerous.'

To: Juliana Abucay
From: Margaret Davis
Date: 11 October 2002

Dear Juliana

That is very good news, we are so happy, thank you. The money will be there at 5pm your time tomorrow, but please use it wisely and not too much at any one time. Please make sure Mama Rosario has money for food and I would like to buy your daughter a gift from Jessica. Tell me if Palabay is coming to Manila to see the police, you know it is important. Where is Evelyn? What do her parents think of her? I think we are very close to getting justice for Steven.

To: Margaret Davis
From: Juliana Abucay
Date: 12 October 2002

Sometimes Palabay say yes he go to police, then he change mind. Mario say he need more time for Palabay, just get Joshua first. Mama Rosario give Evelyn big slap on her face many times and tell her she very bad girl, her family shamed of her. We don't know where is Evelyn now.

I thought this was right: saving Joshua was a priority, and we'd have to work on Palabay later – he might prove to be a hard nut to crack. The idea of the elderly matriarch giving Evelyn what for made me smile. But I still failed to under-stand why Evelyn was not in jail, and how I was able from my small house in Nottinghamshire to get in touch with the people on the ground, whereas the entire PI police force and the mighty British Embassy had failed to make any progress. The frustration was killing me, and at times I felt we would never get there.

One morning while I was folding towels in the bathroom Jessica said something that stopped me in my tracks.

'My mummy helped Arnold bang bang my daddy. My mummy bad lady.'

'Your mummy helped Arnold bang bang your daddy?' I repeated, using a counselling technique I had learnt during my studies, hoping to draw her out more.

'My mummy make my daddy go sleeping. My daddy sleep with Jesus.'

'Your daddy loved you very much, Jessica, and so does your mummy. But you are right, your mummy did a bad thing, and we are sad about that.' I couldn't lie to her, not if she somehow knew the truth. She gazed at me with her large brown eyes and nodded. Then she went back to playing with her My Little Pony. Where had she got this from? Alan and I had been scrupulous about not talking about the case in front of her, so perhaps she had known the truth all along and had not been able to vocalise it until now. Her language was coming on in leaps and bounds. I hoped that this meant she was managing to reconcile it in her mind. Maybe she understood it all better than I did: I felt I would never be able to come to terms with what had happened.

To: Margaret Davis
From: Juliana Abucay
Date: 14 October 2002

I got a problem, the parents of Evelyn change their minds. They want much money for Joshua and they are afraid of the anger of Evelyn, they think she is possessed. This I hear from Mario, so I say me and Jose and his brother, we go to Vasayer and get Joshua, my husband was a policeman once and his brother is a major in the army. I say we have papers we can do this thing, and Evelyn will be arrested. We speak to police and Vasayer, and they want to help. Don't worry Tita it will be all right. Take care!!!!!

I put my head in my hands. This was a blow – we had sent the money and now they were playing hardball. Juliana was clearly trying to show me she had a plan, but I was getting to the point where I was losing faith in her. What were all those exclamation marks about? They didn't fool me; this was not

good news at all. We had had so many reverses and false
hopes since we returned home six weeks earlier, I wasn't sure
I could cope with this rollercoaster any longer. I was also
running out of money – my life savings were almost gone and
I could see that I would have to go back to work. But how
could I, if I was looking after Jessica? I sent a short message
back to Juliana pleading with her to do whatever she could.

The next morning I felt stronger, and emailed Peter
Hawkins. I asked him to use whatever powers he had to
push the police to issue the subpoena against Evelyn – and if
necessary contact the President of the Philippines. 'I am in a
corner, and I must do something,' I wrote. 'Whatever the
risks, I am ready to come back and deal with this myself.
Anything would be better than sitting here getting nowhere.'
I meant it.

To: Margaret Davis
From: Juliana Abucay
Date: 15 October 2002

Evelyn father desperate for money, I talk to him on phone and he
is ready to give Joshua to me. I think this is true and they will be
here by Wednesday. If not plan B is for my sister to pretend to be
social worker and that Joshua is under her care. We try in a nice
way, but if they are bad we will be bad too. I pray that God will
help us.
Always, Juliana

I did not believe either of these solutions would work. I was
exhausted and had run out of ideas, but nevertheless I gave
Juliana details of the embassy telephone numbers and the
means of getting the official documents for Joshua. And I
started looking into flights to Manila. Then, finally, a
breakthrough.

To: Margaret Davis
From: Juliana Abucay
Date: 16 October 2002

Evelyn's father he give Joshua to Jose today. The old man he cry and say he want to see Joshua someday. This we promise and say just for health of Joshua we take him, and he will not forget his Philippine family. Much sorrow in Vasayer when they say goodbye to baby Joshua. More tomorrow, take care, your friend Juliana

Tears sprang to my eyes when I read this. Tears of happiness that Joshua was finally on his way, and sadness for the other grandparents who had the same love and concern for the little boy as we did. How cruel the world was, that we had the money and resources to care for him and they were to live without him. Evelyn's father was an ancient, wizened old man and I doubted he would ever see his grandson again. I immediately emailed the embassy in Manila with the good news.

To: Margaret Davis
From: Peter Hawkins
Date: 16 October 2002

Message received loud and clear – congratulations! The Ambassador will see the Chief of Police tomorrow morning to push things along with regard to Hernandez' report and the arrest of Evelyn and Palabay. I look forward to meeting Jose and Joshua.
Sincerely
Peter

Things started happening very quickly after that. I gave Peter the address of the village where Palabay was hiding, and details of how to find Evelyn in the squatters' compound. The following day Jose and Joshua arrived in Manila and I wired more money for Evelyn's parents, organised a visa for Jose, and bought air tickets for the two of them. To my surprise I received a call from the ambassador himself assuring me that the police were ready to arrest Evelyn and Palabay.

That afternoon Jose telephoned. I could hardly believe that he was sitting holding Joshua on his knee, and I excitedly called to Jessica. I gave her the phone. 'Say hello to baby Joshua.' She was stunned for a moment, then couldn't stop talking.

'Joshua, this is Jessica. You come to me soon, I know. I have special things for you and food, and a nice bedroom and everything.' She listened to whatever noises he was making on the other end, and gave me the receiver. Her face was one huge smile.

'Joshua is happy to come to us, Nana.'

To: Margaret Davis
From: Juliana Abucay
Date: 19 October 2002

At last everything is fine. Josh's grandpa said to Evelyn that he gave Joshua to you and Evelyn cried. But the father say she already abandon Joshua and it was her fault, what life could she give to her baby when she is in jail. He say he ashamed of her, and she never can come to their village again. I tell her father what you tell me, that you always tell the children of the kind thing they did, that they let you have Joshua to give him good future, and they always remember their Filipino family with good heart.
Yours, Juliana.

Four days later all the papers were in order and Joshua and Jose were on their way. It was six weeks since we had returned from Manila and I was worn out with negotiations, worry and the effort of staying cheerful for Jessica's sake.

The night before they were to arrive I sent Jessica to stay with my sister over the road – I felt very fragile and tearful and I knew she would be confused by the flurry of emotions that were sure to be in the air. Alan and I drove to Heathrow and spent the night in a hotel, to be sure we were on time in the morning. I got very little sleep, what with all the excitement, apprehension and exhaustion.

Then at last we were there, waiting in the arrivals lounge. It was a chilly autumn morning, and I was prepared, clutching a small bag containing trousers, a woolly hat and a warm jacket.

We could see from the flight indicator that the plane had landed, and we waited anxiously as the passengers filed slowly through the arrivals gate. No sign of them. Finally, all the passengers from that flight had come through. No Jose, no Joshua. I began to cry, feeling utterly defeated. 'Something's gone wrong, Alan. What can we do?' I looked around frantically. Suddenly there was an announcement over the tannoy.

'*Would the family meeting Joshua Alston Davis and Jose Abucay please go through to the immigration office.*' I panicked, terrified that they would not be allowed into the country. Perhaps the papers were faulty. Alan took my hand and led me to the office.

'Let's stay calm, Marg. We've done nothing wrong.' I couldn't help myself; I felt on edge and tearful.

The immigration officer was unsmiling.

'Can you tell us why a Filipino male is escorting a minor with a British passport?'

'Jose Abucay is a distant relative of our daughter-in-law. Our son has died and she has given us permission to have the child.'

'To have the child? That sounds unusual.'

'For a holiday. We have her signatures on these forms. Mr

Abucay is escorting the child to us and will also stay with us for a holiday.' I produced the original passport application, the immigration exit visa and all sorts of other documents that I had, luckily, brought along with me.

'Thank you. Would you mind waiting here while I talk to my colleagues?'

My God, this was like being back in the Philippines. Again I was filled with that creeping sense that we were criminals. However, at least we didn't have to wait five hours this time. After half an hour we were told we could go back to the arrivals hall and receive our visitors. Put the flags out. I couldn't get there fast enough.

There was Joshua in Jose's arms. He was wearing a dirty Babygro that was too small for him, the legs cut off at the ankles to reveal brown legs and a large pair of British Airways socks. He looked at me with frightened eyes, but I held out my arms to him and smiled. 'Hello, Joshua.' There was a moment's silence, when he seemed unsure of who I was or what he should do, then a flicker of recognition passed over his face and suddenly he was clinging to my neck like a limpet. I wrapped my arms around this small, frightened bundle and whispered, 'I'll keep you safe, my love. I'll keep you safe now.' It was wonderful just to have Steven's son in my arms after all we had been through.

'I can't thank you enough, Jose,' I said. I knew what a big thing it had been for Jose to leave his country to bring this baby to us.

'God helped us, Ma'am.'

We put the clothes we'd brought on Joshua's thin, sore body. I had not been prepared for the shock of seeing him. I could see he was covered in mosquito bites, many of which were oozing pus.

'Has he seen a doctor, Jose?'

'Yes, Ma'am, I took him two days ago. He has antibiotics

for these wounds. Look at this red mark around his ankle – he has been tied up to a tree.'

Joshua did not cry, just stared and stared, following Jose with his eyes as if afraid he would lose him. I could see how much he had grown to trust this big, kind Filipino man.

'Where are his shoes?' I asked.

'Only these, Ma'am,' said Jose, handing me a pair of squeaky Batman flip-flops.

We made the three-hour journey back home in silence. Joshua slept, and we were all wrapped up in our own thoughts; Jose wondering, no doubt, how long he would be able to stay in the UK and whether he'd be able to get his family over here; Alan, perhaps, thinking about suddenly being a father to two small children. And as for me, I was amazed and grateful to have Steven's cherished son at long last, but still bursting with grief for my own son.

12
I Start to Fall Apart

At last I had both Steven's children safe at home with me. To a casual observer it may have seemed that I would now have been able to relax, settle into looking after my new family, and let the authorities in the Philippines continue with the case against Evelyn. Unfortunately the reality was far more complicated, and I was totally unprepared for the emotional and practical challenges that were about to hit me with the force of a high-speed train.

Joshua cried almost continuously for the first fortnight. The sound was terrible – high-pitched, relentless. It was an alien sound to me, very different from the cries I remembered from my own children. The tired cries, the hungry cries, the wanting-attention cries: all those I had learnt to interpret and deal with. I knew I had been a loving, competent mother – and with Jessica I felt I had been making real progress. She was responding to me, opening up, and beginning to blossom. But Joshua was pre-verbal, and try as I might I could not communicate with him. It was clear that the little thing was desperately confused and unhappy, yet when I tried to comfort him he pushed me away. I came to rely on Jose to take charge of his every need, feeding and changing him, carrying him around and comforting him. It seemed that the only time he stopped crying was when he was eating or drinking. I never saw him laugh, or even smile.

Jessica arrived back from my sister Gillian's house on the first afternoon we had Joshua. Full of excitement, she rushed up to him and threw her arms around him, talking nineteen to the dozen about us, her room, her new toys and friends. It had only been two months since he had seen her, but there was no spark of recognition in his eyes. She hesitated, bewildered. He started to wail again and put his arms up to Jose to be picked up. Jessica ran up to her room in tears. 'He just needs some time, my pet. Remember when you first arrived, it was confusing for you too,' I tried to reassure her.

This became a pattern. Jessie would try so hard to communicate with him, offering him toys and books to hold, trying out both English and Tagalog words, yet he gave nothing back. His expression was blank, he would shake his head at her, and she would feel rebuffed once again. It broke my heart to watch it. The tentative steps forward we had managed to achieve in building her confidence dissipated almost overnight. Her behaviour gradually changed, and the nightmares and anxiety returned. Josh was sleeping in a borrowed cot in Jose's room, and Jessica now wanted to be back in our bedroom with us. She also seemed to be afraid of Jose.

As for me, I was on a knife-edge. Desperate to keep going through the day, I tried to focus on the practical side of things, shopping for milk, baby food and warm clothes for Jose and Joshua, and concentrating on Jessica's wellbeing and bringing back her confidence. I had a task to do, a new job, and it was essential to keep going. But I could see I was failing at this, and despite my efforts to hold my emotions together I was on the verge of tears all the time. I felt I was falling apart. My sister was a huge support, and would arrive every morning to help with Jessica, but every time I heard Joshua's piercing cry I felt an explosion in my brain that would knock me sideways. I wanted to get out of the house, anywhere, just run – and sometimes I did. It got to the point where I could not bear to look at him or touch him. How could this be? I had got what I wanted, hadn't I? 'Get a grip,' I would tell myself. 'Think about what this child has been through. Of course he's going to have trouble settling down.' I had done the right thing by this little boy, and I was going to take care of him somehow. I thought back over my two months' fight to get him, and asked myself why I wasn't more pleased to have him here with us at last. Then it struck me. I didn't want him; I wanted Steven. The guilt of these feelings racked my soul. I did not understand what was happening to me, and I had no idea what to do to help myself.

Alan at all times stood by his promise to help with the children. Jose would take care of Joshua's day-to-day needs, and Alan would be there to comfort me and remind me of all the good times we had with Steven. 'We owe it to him to keep his children safe. In fact, do you remember promising him this?' I did. It was just after my own mother had died, and we were talking with Steven in the gazebo one evening.

'You had better get your affairs in order, Mum,' Steve had said. 'I don't want to have to return to the UK to clear things up if anything happened to you.'

'And vice versa,' was my sharp reply.

He looked pensive. 'What would you do if that happened?'

'Simple. I would support your wife and children in the Philippines and make sure they came to the UK for education.'

'I do worry about that, you know. Evelyn doesn't agree with education – if it was left up to her they'd be ignorant and illiterate.' I knew this. Steven had given her money to enrol Jessie in the local Montessori school, and believed she was attending it. One morning he took her to school himself, complete with packed lunch, and was shocked and mortified to discover that the teachers did not know the little girl.

'Well, that won't happen. Not in my lifetime,' I stated categorically. Never did I imagine that I would actually need to carry out this promise.

Nevertheless it was hard, and I went to my GP for sleeping

pills. I had to escape to somewhere and I was just so dog tired. The doctor asked me if I had experienced suicidal thoughts. 'No, of course not,' I said confidently, thinking, 'I will if I don't get my hands on these tablets, mate.' The truth was, if I admitted my feelings of despair and hopelessness at this point I would be at risk of losing the children. So I took steps to find out what help was available from the state. I knew of a local family who had adopted a Romanian child – they had been given all sorts of support. Shouldn't we be eligible for something? It would lighten the load.

While this was going on I was being bombarded with requests for a visa from Jose's wife. I had promised her that she and her youngest daughter would be able to come over and join her husband, but I was in no fit state to organise anything now. The process of getting Joshua had stretched my organisational skills to the limit, and I needed a break. Besides, if I couldn't cope with having Alan, Jessica, Jose and Joshua in the house, how on earth was I going to deal with two more? I kept telling myself to keep calm, to keep sane, to take things one step at a time. Juliana was the key to getting Palabay and Evelyn to trial and I still needed her help.

But Juliana was starting to get frightened.

To: Margaret Davis
From: Juliana Abucay
Date: 2 November 2002

Dear Tita Margaret
I really afraid of Evelyn, she is desperate, I think she know her life is useless now. I stay with my mother, I can't go out because I worry Evelyn is crazy she want to kill me too. She is now selling her body to anyone, she have no money. I miss Jose please give him my hug.
Yours, Juliana

To: Juliana Abucay
From: Margaret Davis
Date: 2 November 2002

Of course Evelyn is crazy, she killed my son. There is nothing I
would like more than to have you and your daughter Lina to stay
here with us, and we will certainly need you here when I have to
go to the trial. I am trying to sort things out. Have you both got
passports? Do not be afraid of Evelyn. Jose is well and sends his
love, let me know a time you can chat on-line and I will make sure
he can be there.
Your friend, Margaret

To: Margaret Davis
From: Juliana Abucay
Date: 3 November 2002

I wish she get arrested as soon as possible so she can't hurt
anyone. There is a police report, and Evelyn saw a copy and said it
was a fake. Deep in her mind I know she is afraid and bothered.
I get my passport soon, thank you. Juliana

I heard around that time from a friend of Steve's that Evelyn
was being given legal aid by a public lawyer who ran a radio
station in Angeles. This worried me, because they would
possibly try to strengthen her case against me, or Juliana and
Jose, for kidnap. I had tried to call Evelyn on her mobile
phone so that she could have some contact with her children,
and so I could reassure her that they were doing well, but I
could never get through. I guessed she had a new number.
Instead, I asked Steve's colleagues to pass on my number to
Evelyn and ask her to call. There were plenty of people in the
office who would know people who could contact her. I
thought I would be able to pacify her somehow and find out
what she was up to.

To: Margaret Davis
From: Christian Aguera Attorney
Date: 4 November 2002

Dear Mrs Davis
We write to advise you that the trial of Adoray and Dagami is on
12 November. Your presence is required to give evidence. Please
advise.

In a panic I called the British Embassy. What should I do?
While I had been prepared to risk kidnap charges to rescue
Joshua, was it really necessary for me to come to testify when
I had already given a sworn affidavit to the court? I was
worried too as the Iraq conflict had just begun and there had
recently been bomb scares in Manila – not to mention an
outbreak of meningitis in the capital city. But if I had
expected solid advice I didn't get it: the embassy told me
it was my call. In truth I was exhausted and simply couldn't
face going over. It was all I could do to get through the days
and gradually gather supporting documents and letters of
invitation to help Juliana and her daughter get to the UK. So
I asked my lawyers to appear instead of me.

I had still had no call from Evelyn. I felt she should have
been concerned about her children: surely any mother would
want to know how they were doing? I was in fact very
concerned, not only because of what they had been through,
but because of how they were behaving. Before Joshua
arrived I had fond ideas of him settling in after a few weeks
and, like Jessica, starting to eat a normal healthy diet and
react as any other fourteen-month-old should do. These
happy-family visions were rapidly fading, and although I
still felt strangely repelled by Joshua I was deeply worried
about his lack of routine and poor diet.

Every evening Jose would prepare a quantity of white rice

and noodles, and these would be fed to the child at odd times during the next day. Jessica also seemed to be regressing, refusing the new types of food I had painfully managed to get her to accept, and insisting on eating the same rice-and-noodle mixture. At least Joshua was eating, that was something – indeed, he would devour vast quantities of food and drink. Yet I knew he needed a balanced diet. I also couldn't cope with the fact that he had no kind of routine at all: I was used to babies his age waking at seven, having a short nap in the morning and a longer one after lunch, then bedtime at about six. I used to play with my children at home in the morning, or take them to the shops, and in the afternoon to the park. Frankly, if children don't know where they stand then there's chaos in the house – and, if nothing else, I believe that adults need to know when they can switch off. Jose's way was to do everything for Joshua, and he carried him around with him constantly. I was kind and loving with my children, but I wouldn't rush to pick them up if they fell over or cried: I always attempted to build their confidence and independence in different ways. So I inwardly rebelled against what I saw as both a casual and overbearing attitude to child-rearing, but I bit my tongue, knowing that it was not my place to criticise the customs of another culture. I would get my way eventually, but it would take time and I did not want to insult Jose by talking out of turn.

'Jose, this rice is very nice and Joshua likes it, but do you think we could try to make some other food for him?' I tried to be tactful one day. 'I remember many delicious dishes we had in the Philippines – rice pudding with coconut milk, chicken adobo, mixed vegetables. Do you know how to cook them?'

'Yes, Ma'am. I can give you a list of food to get and I will try to cook.' This was progress, and I eagerly did as he asked. That evening I'm pleased to say we had our first family tea together since Joshua's arrival, and I felt we were getting somewhere. Jose was doing his best to please me, and the children wolfed the food down. At least they weren't starving.

After the meal I felt so much better about Joshua that I volunteered to take him upstairs to bed. 'Alan and I will bath the children tonight, Jose.'

We watched them play, reasonably happily, in the bath together. As I got Josh dressed in his bedtime Babygro, I looked at his tummy. It didn't look right.

'Alan, just look at Josh a minute. Do you see anything odd?'

'No, I don't think so. What do you see?'

'His stomach. Look at the shape of it, he reminds me of those malnourished African children you see on the telly.' It was true. His belly was enormous, but his chest and legs looked painfully thin.

'He's just had a huge meal, perhaps that's why. But if you're worried, take him to the doctor.'

'I will. I just have a feeling there's something not quite right with this kid. He's so miserable all the time, he cries constantly. And have you noticed he's always dribbling? Perhaps he's got a virus?'

The next day I took Joshua to our GP.

'What seems to be the problem?' he asked. I pointed out Josh's distended tummy, and mentioned his runny nose.

'He always seems to have a cold, but he hasn't got a temperature. I can't take him out without a bib on because he dribbles so much. And look at his eyes, they seem to be full of tears even when he's not crying. Which admittedly isn't often.'

'It looks like this young man is teething,' said the doctor with a smile. 'Give him some Calpol every four hours and he should weather it.'

'Are you sure? He has recently returned from Asia – is there a chance it could be something else?'

'Well, just to be extra-sure let's give him some antibiotics. Come back if he doesn't improve after a week.'

I had to accept this, and I tried to calm down. I had done as much as I could, and Jose dutifully gave Joshua the pain-relieving medicine and the antibiotics for a week. It was a worrying time, and I could see no immediate improvement. I'd never forgive myself if something happened to Joshua.

There was a local nursery I had been hoping to get Jessica into, and finally a place had come up. It was a five-minute walk from our house, and I felt it would be a lovely environment for her to start her schooling. She was ready for more creative play – sand, clay, paint – that I couldn't provide at home, and the nursery had a wonderful outside space too. We wanted her to start to socialise with other children – many of whom were mixed-race like her – and we also felt it would be healthy to get her away from Joshua's constant whimpering. However, it was clear from the first few days that she would be one of those children who take a long time to settle in. Every time I tried to leave she would burst into tears, and try to follow me out. She was happy if she could see me, but if I even moved into an adjoining room she would become anxious and fretful. The staff listened to what I told them about her recent history, and agreed that I could stay for the two hours each morning until she felt more comfortable.

It was on one of these mornings, shortly after our visit to the doctor, that I had a panic call from my sister. Gillian was in the habit of taking over from me in the mornings to give Jose a break, and would regularly wash, dress and feed Josh.

'Come back quickly, Margaret. It's Josh.'

We had only just arrived at the nursery, but I turned round

and went straight back home, leaving an unhappy Jessica to fend for herself that morning.

'What is it?' I called as soon as I got in the house, terrified of what I might hear. Gill was upstairs, bending over Joshua, who was lying on the changing mat.

'Look in his nappy,' she said simply.

What I saw took my breath away. There, in the nappy, a tangled mass of thick, brownish-pink worms wriggled and squirmed. They looked like earthworms. My gorge rose and I almost retched.

'My God. Wrap up the nappy, I'll get him dressed. Let's go down the doctor's straight away.' Within fifteen minutes we were there, and the receptionist took us into the surgery immediately.

'What an astonishing sight!' the doctor exclaimed. 'I never imagined I would ever see intestinal worms like these. They must be some tropical variety.' I wasn't interested in or intrigued about what they were, I just wanted Joshua fixed.

'What do we do?'

'Yes of course.' He roused himself. 'I'll book him into the isolation unit at the hospital, and I expect they'll analyse these little devils and find out what the treatment is.'

I spent seven days in that hospital with Joshua. The little thing looked so small and vulnerable tucked up in a standard-size hospital bed, a glucose drip and an antibiotic drip attached to a cannula in his wrist and a tube inserted through his nose to draw fluid from his stomach. Another nasal tube led to a bag hanging above his shoulder, drawing out what looked like minute green threads. They were newly hatched eggs. Samples were taken of all his bodily fluids and sent off for analysis, and we waited for the verdict from the tropical diseases specialist. We did not have long to wait, for on the second day a group of student doctors trooped in with a consultant.

'This is a child who is infected with a tropical parasite,' announced the consultant. 'From early tests it appears to be the nematode *Ascaris lumbricoides*, rarely seen in Britain but in fact fairly common throughout the developing world.'

'What is the lifecycle?' one of the students asked.

'The adult worms live in the small intestine and eggs are passed in the faeces. A single female can produce up to 200,000 eggs each day, which explains how in areas where sanitation is poor – particularly where human waste is used as fertilizer – the infection rate is massive.'

'So the eggs somehow get onto food?'

'Correct – as I said, poor hygiene, dirty utensils, you can imagine. The eggs are resistant to extremes of temperature so are not easily eradicated. They hatch in the small intestine, the juvenile penetrates the small intestine and enters the circulatory system, and eventually the juvenile worm enters the lungs. From here it gets into the air passages of the lungs and thence into the pharynx where it is swallowed. When it is in the small intestine the juvenile grows into an adult worm.'

'What are the symptoms, doctor?' I cut in here. This was my grandson he was talking about, yet it felt as if Alan and I were being ignored, and I wondered if there was anything I ought to have spotted. My guilt reflex, as you may have noticed, works overtime.

'It depends on how far advanced the infestation is,' the consultant explained. 'The migration of the larvae through the lungs causes the blood vessels of the lungs to haemorrhage, and there is an inflammatory response accompanied by excess fluid. The resulting accumulation of fluids in the lungs can result in a kind of pneumonia, and this can be fatal – although not in this case.' Ah, that would explain the constantly runny nose, the leaking eyes, the dribbling. The consultant continued: 'The large size of the adult worms also presents problems, especially if the worms physically block the gastrointestinal tract. *Ascaris* is notorious for its ability to migrate within the small intestine, and when a large worm begins to move from organ to organ there is not much that can stop it. They may, alarmingly, sometimes migrate forward through the intestinal tract, either to be vomited up or to emerge through the nose. More seriously, if they enter the windpipe they may cause suffocation. Instances have been reported in which *Ascaris* have blocked the bile duct or the pancreatic duct, or in which the worms have actually penetrated the wall of the intestine. If this happens the patient would be likely to die of peritonitis or blood poisoning.'

This was disgusting. I shuddered and sat down on the chair next to Joshua's bed. Even the students looked a bit squeamish. Yet another horror to have emerged from that country, I thought.

'Joshua is a very lucky little boy. The mortality rate for children is very high, for without treatment they can quickly become dehydrated and at the same time their lungs fatally congested. I suggest the whole family be checked just to ensure we eradicate these worms completely.'

Eventually Joshua was pronounced clear of worms, and we were able to take him home. Jessica's tests, on the other hand, showed that she was carrying not the *Ascaris* worm, but tuberculosis antibodies – she had been exposed to the disease and could potentially develop it. So she wasn't out of the woods either, and had to swallow thick red medicine twice a day for the next four months, attending a clinic once a week for a weight check and dosage adjustment. She hated it, but like the sweetheart she is, did as she was told obediently.

I wondered what else was lurking in their systems, what physical conditions were lying hidden, preparing to ambush us. Medical problems I could just about cope with, though, and I knew my main task was to concentrate on their health and wellbeing. What kept me awake at night was anxiety about whatever dormant psychological wounds these children had suffered: what would emerge as these two innocents grew up? I could only guess, and try meanwhile to get through each day. When, I wondered, would I be able to step off this rollercoaster and come to terms with my own grief and loss? I was too old for this, I felt, and at night would fall into bed with just one thought in my head. *Stop the world, I want to get off.*

13
No Help

Joshua's health continued to improve slowly. Jose did what he could to help, but he was becoming glum and miserable, clearly missing his wife and family. The weather closed in, and we spent time indoors – this was frustrating for the children, who were used to running around outside. Jessica was very unsure about being anywhere she could not see me, and would still sit on her haunches, observing and not joining in to play. She was also still wary of Jose and would avoid being alone in a room with him. Then one night as she was settling into bed she asked, 'Why is Arnold in this house with us?'

I froze, for a mad moment wondering if she was seeing things. Then I realised she must be confusing Jose with her mother's lover, presumably because he was a Filipino male.

'Arnold is not here, my sweet, he is a long way away. In prison.'

'Who is the man with Joshua?'

'That's Jose. You know Jose. He is a good man, he helped find Josh for us, and he helps us look after Josh. Jose is not Arnold, he doesn't know Arnold. Jose is our friend.'

She took a lot of convincing. The memories were becoming blurred in her mind, and what remained was fear and insecurity.

'Mummy loves Arnold, not Daddy Steven. She no love me and Joshua,' Jessica said in a small voice. She would say this often, and each time I would gather her to me and try to reassure her. 'Mummy does love Jessica and Joshua, but she can't be with you now. Jessica is a lucky girl to have Nana and Papa and Joshua and lots of friends in England.' It was so hard to say the right things to this little girl, sometimes I felt I was walking on eggshells – it would be so easy to say the wrong thing and mess with her mind. I expressed my concerns to Alan – were we doing the right thing? What should we be telling them? What if we got it wrong? What sort of psychological impact should we be worried about causing? Should we have left them with their family in the Philippines? Should they still at least be with their mother? But as usual he cut to what was important: 'These are Steven's children. They need love and care, and right now they're with the best people to provide that. The alternatives are too frightening to think about.'

Nevertheless, I asked the GP what to do, and he arranged counselling for Jessica and gave me some ideas about what to say when she wanted to talk. I was worried that Jessica did not cry noisily like other children, who sobbed out loud or whined while they cried. Her tears always fell silently, huge drops welling up from her big brown eyes as if the painful memories were simply spilling out the only way they could. Tears that were the outward sign of overflowing feelings that she did not understand and had no way of dealing with. She would have had so many memories. She had seen her daddy lying lifeless in a glasstopped coffin as though just asleep; she had seen her mother cavorting naked with her lover. She had seen the gun in Arnold's house that killed her father, she was there at the drunken parties her mother had in Steven's house when he was at work. She knew 'Mummy did not buy her and Joshua food' and that 'Daddy Steven took her shopping when he was at home'. She knew 'Mummy did not love Daddy Steven'. Did that mean Mummy did not love her either? All these things this little girl had told me. What more had she experienced that I did not hear about? How I hated Evelyn at these times for putting her children through such things. The counsellor told me about other symptoms of trauma, and I ticked them all off in my mind: recurring night terrors and nightmares; thrashing while asleep; forgetfulness; excessive belligerence and shyness; extreme clinginess, and stomach-aches.

As a result of these sessions I became more aware of Jessica's body language. She loved music and would beg to watch MTV, but I was disturbed at the way she danced. At the age of four she mimicked perfectly the lascivious moves of a bar dancer, throwing her head and hair back suggestively, touching herself seductively and moving as if in a trance. I bought parenting books, realising I needed a crash course on handling difficult and traumatised children, and learnt that it is more important to praise good behaviour than to reprimand bad behaviour. I decided that dancing was OK, and made it a game for her to play with Joshua: we would put on the same music and I would suggest Jessie copy the girls on the TV, rather than the hookers and bar girls she had watched from an early age. For Christmas I bought her a DVD of pop-music dance moves for children in the hope that she would adopt a different style.

Talk was a big healer. Jessie would ask, 'Do you love my mummy?' by way of a test. 'Yes darling, I *used* to love her very much,' I'd reply. This was the truth, and I would remind her of some of the happier times we'd had together. I would always finish by telling her that 'Mummy chooses to be with Arnold and it is not your fault. When she is ready she can come here to us and share all your nice things.'

This was true – if Evelyn was innocent, I would invite her to come and stay with us. I needed to give Jessica positive hope, because there is only so much hard truth a small child can take. She had her own preconceived ideas about her mother that she would only rationalise when she was older and able to understand. I never let Jessica see my anger towards her mother. In a book about explaining death to children, I had learnt that I should be as matter-of-fact as possible, and describe what has happened briefly and without too much emotion. This was advice that I tried to follow when dealing with all her many questions, remembering that this was not just the death of her father she was dealing with; she was grieving for the loss of her mummy, her friends, her family, her home, her culture and her whole being. I reassured her constantly that I loved her, and would hug and tickle her. She loved physical contact, but another odd thing was that she rarely laughed naturally. She had a false giggle that to me suggested that she wanted to laugh, but did not yet feel free or relaxed enough.

At other times I felt Jessica had sorted everything out and come to terms with it. Like the time I took her to the pharmacy after I had accidentally burnt her hand with some hot coffee. The pharmacist took her hand and held it kindly, talking of creams and bandages. Jessica responded by saying in a matter-of-fact tone I recognised as my own, 'My mummy killed my daddy, you know. She is a bad mummy.' The poor man looked at me in astonishment, and I nodded at him, not wanting to confirm this out loud, but not wanting to deny it either. This became quite a refrain with Jessica, and whenever she came into contact with new people she would proffer the same information. I could see she was trying to reconcile it in her mind, as if by repeating it she would gradually come to understand it, and make it real and normal.

To: Margaret Davis
From: Christian Aguera, Attorney
Date: 12 November 2002

We have received a summons requiring your presence before 3rd Assistant City Prosecutor on 12th and 19th November. As today is

12th November and we receive the summons only today we ask
that you confirm you will fly over on 19th November to aid in the
investigation. We also inform you that the Prosecutor's Office in
Makati City has begun the preliminary investigation to determine
whether or not to charge Evelyn or Palabay for the crime of
murder committed against Steven.

Very truly yours.

'Not again,' I groaned to Alan. 'I don't think I ought to go
with the threat of arrest for kidnap hanging over me.'

'It's a Catch-22 situation, isn't it?' he agreed. 'They need
you to be there to give evidence to put Evelyn away, but until
she's put away you're not safe to be there.'

But did I really need to be there? I contacted all the usual
people, and was told that indeed my lawyers ought to get on
with this themselves – they had enough information; they
were just being lazy. Meanwhile I was working hard on
Juliana's behalf, writing letters and finding all the supporting
documents necessary to get her a visa. She was becoming
more anxious every day.

To: Margaret Davis
From: Juliana Abucay
Date: 20 November 2002

I now hear that Evelyn does voodoo on you. She has model doll of
you and she do bad things to it, maybe to me too. Tita Margaret,
please take care this is real and I very afraid for you. I hope I can
come soon to you, my life is very sad by myself.

Juliana

'Oh, for goodness' sake!' I exclaimed to Alan on reading this.
'I'm too scientific to believe in this witchcraft nonsense.'

'Juliana's scared though, Margaret. Whether or not it's
real and whether or not it works, we must help her to get

here soon.' I knew he was right, and I was not going to go back on my promise, but it seemed that between our authorities in the UK and those in the Philippines, things were taking a long time. I hoped Juliana would stay safe until the visa was ready.

To: Margaret Davis
From: Juliana Abucay
Date: 29 November 2002

Please let me know when the visa is OK. Evelyn is now living in the squatters compound, she has many bad friends. Why she not arrested, I don't understand.
Yours, Juliana

That was a good question – what about the subpoena? When I dug a little further, I was angry (but not surprised) to discover that it had been sent to Steven's house. Evelyn had moved out weeks ago. The frustration was killing me – they had her new address in the squatters' compound. Not only that, a subpoena was one thing, just a document requiring her to give evidence. But why was there still no warrant for her arrest? Surely they had enough evidence? I called the embassy, I asked people at Steve's office, I hassled my lawyers, I emailed the police station. I even wrote to Ken Clarke, but all I ever received was a printed acknowledge-ment card. I wanted to know what had happened about Arnold Adoray's and Alex Dagami's application for bail – and, if it had failed, when the trial would be. There was so much evidence against Evelyn, and three affidavits connect-ing her with Arnold – how could it be ignored? I was starting to wonder if the police themselves could be involved in all this. I couldn't ask Juliana to find out anything: she was desperately frightened as it was.

To: Margaret Davis
From: Juliana Abucay
Date: 15 December 2002

Evelyn went to our house again with three men. She was looking for me and said to my niece if it wasn't for me she would have no problem. Even my friends now text me and ask if I am kidnapper, what happened, and they gave these men my address. I must go to my sister's house in the provinces and hide. Don't tell Jose this, I don't want him to worry. If Evelyn can kill Steven she can do the same to me, I think you are right she is evil. Do I need to go to embassy for visa or do I wait for their call?

To: Juliana Abucay
From: Margaret Davis
Date: 17 December 2002

I think the visa is nearly ready, the embassy will call you. Please be very careful and try to keep cheerful, you will soon be with us. Try to find out what you can about Evelyn and tell my lawyer she is threatening you.

To: Margaret Davis
From: Juliana Abucay
Date: 18 December 2002

I thank God for bringing you into my life, I now have call that visa is ready, so now all I need is ticket. I hear people say that Evelyn and Arnold get money to escape to another country??

To: Juliana Abucay
From: Margaret Davis
Date: 19 December 2002

Your ticket is waiting in your name at the British Airways office, but I could not get a flight for you until 18 January – all other flights are booked because of Chinese New Year. Before you leave please tell Mama Rosario and Aurora and Maria that when Evelyn is in jail I will be back for the trial and I will bring them gifts. Don't worry about Evelyn, she has no money and she will not be able to escape.

Poor Juliana was not happy about this, but there was nothing more I could do to get her to the UK earlier. Meanwhile we were getting on with preparations for Christmas. I had little heart for it this year, but for the sake of the children I went through the motions and tried to put on a good show. The family rallied round, aware that I was not my normal capable, positive self. Jessica was still jumpy, hiding each time the doorbell rang 'in case it is Arnold'; Joshua was crying less and sleeping more, but he rarely smiled. It was around this time that my daughter Lucy started taking Joshua each weekend, and Gill had Jessica. This gave me some respite, but I felt guilty that I could not cope with them, and my heart would sink when they returned on Sunday evening, knowing that Monday would be the start of another identical week: a daily struggle to make progress with the children, afraid to say the wrong thing, unsure of myself, waiting for news of Evelyn, the unbearable frustration of not being able to do anything. The months seemed to stretch out ahead of me, and I felt a lowering sense of gloom that I couldn't shake off.

One evening the three of us were alone in the house. It was already dark, and they'd had their tea. We were watching TV on the sofa and Joshua's head was lolling against my side – he had nodded off. I was so tired, so drained, so close to giving up. Getting through the day was such a struggle, and sitting there that evening I was suddenly filled with an overwhelming sense of peace, and the certain knowledge that I had it in my power, at that moment, to solve everything. It would be so easy to take them to Steven. I would simply stifle them with cushions and swallow the little bottle of sleeping pills I kept upstairs. Where was the crime in that? I would be saving us all a lifetime of suffering. Could I do it?

Then I felt Jessica's little hand in mine, and she said, 'I love you, Nana.' I knew then that of course I could never do it. Could never deprive these precious creatures of life. Tears sprang to my eyes.

'I'm going to look after you, Jessica. I'm going to protect and shelter you until you are old enough to . . .' I faltered, and didn't finish the sentence. As soon as you are old enough to be able to face what has happened to you, to us, to your father. I felt hot anger rising in me at Evelyn. 'It's OK, Nana. Don't cry.' Jessica stroked my cheek, and I buried my face in her smooth, black hair. Evelyn might be walking free now but I was not going to give up until she had been called to account for the destruction she had caused. I had to live in order to see my mission through.

As Juliana waited for her plane tickets, the other people over there who had helped me started to become restless. They were jealous that Jose and his wife were able to start a new life in the UK (although this was not what I had promised, merely a holiday as a thankyou for rescuing Joshua) and were agitating for the same things – more money, and sponsorship to come to us.

To: Margaret Davis
From: Juliana Abucay
Date: 1 January 2003

Dear Tita
Rosario and some others want to withdraw their statements. They feel angry I leave them here and they not trust you give

them more money. I say you give more gifts when Evelyn in
prison and when this thing is finished, but they not believe. Sorry
for this, Juliana

This was blackmail, and I was not going to be drawn. It was
becoming more urgent than ever to get the case wrapped up.
It was the start of a new year and I renewed my calls to my
lawyers, the embassy and my MP to put a bomb under the
Philippine so-called judicial system. Surely someone, somewhere, could get answers. It seemed that the minute we had
left the country everything had ground to a halt. Maybe it
really was time to return. Meanwhile I attempted to keep
Juliana positive and pacify her contacts. If they withdrew
their statements we were finished, but I realised there was
little I could do.

To: Juliana Abucay
From: Margaret Davis
Date: 2 January 2003

Juliana, you must make them understand the situation. I have
not betrayed them, I am grateful for their help in getting justice
for my murdered son and for their bravery in telling the truth I
gave them gifts. It is not easy to bring foreign nationals to the UK
and as you know it takes time and is expensive. You and Jose are
in a different position because of your deep involvement in the
case, but even you only have a 6-month visa.

To: Margaret Davis
From: Juliana Abucay
Date: 3 January 2003

I know, but this is difficult. I get bad texts from people and we
have arguments all the time. I worry that if they withdraw their

statement Evelyn will be free and then she make case against me
for kidnap. Thinking of all this making me ill. Another thing is I
hear Evelyn has some share document and she says she will be
rich.

I knew what this was – a share certificate relating to Steven's
company, the one I couldn't find when we cleared his room.
It wasn't hers, and she had said she would pass it to her
lawyer. Obviously she hadn't. Yet another thing I had to try
to get hold of: if the company did well, this would be my
grandchildren's inheritance.

To: Juliana Abucay
From: Margaret Davis
Date: 4 January 2003

Evelyn signed papers allowing the children to come here. You did
not kidnap them and she cannot claim this. Try not to worry, you
will be here soon. As for Mama Rosario and the others, my
message is the same. When we have a conclusion I will arrange
a gift for their efforts. I will not be blackmailed, and if they
withdraw their statements I can do nothing but the court may
go after them for contempt. Remember this is a very bad crime,
people must not get away with murder. If you want to give me
their mobile phone numbers I can contact them directly. Take
care, Margaret.

Towards the end of January Juliana and her daughter duly
arrived, and were reunited with Jose. It was nice to have the
house buzzing with chatter and laughter, and suddenly I had
much more help with the children. However, after a few days
Jose approached me, looking serious.

'Ma'am, I think Juliana and me, we should go for advice
to the asylum centre.' I looked at him blankly, failing to
understand what he was saying. Asylum?

'There is a price on my head for helping a Westerner put my fellow Filipinos into prison and for the taking of Joshua. Juliana too in trouble. We both worry, please, Ma'am, we need to go for advice.' I did not have the strength to object. The next day they went to the asylum centre in Croydon – I didn't see them for two weeks.

As the door slammed behind them I turned to face Alan. Now I would be alone with the children for the first time since Joshua arrived. Alan would be going out to work and I was to be the mummy.

'How am I going to cope?' I sighed.

'We'll be all right, you'll see,' he replied. 'Let's take this one step at a time. Jessie's at nursery, and she goes to Gill's at weekends. We need to find some help with Joshua – he'll be two soon, don't they do nursery places for kids of that age? He definitely needs socialising a little more.'

'Yes, I'm looking forward to getting Joshua into more of a routine. He's in this country now, and at nineteen months old he still can't speak a word of English. I'd like him to grow up into a strong, independent little chap. Perhaps it's for the best that we'll be on our own for a bit, I was starting to feel out of control in my own house with such a crowd.'

'I've been wondering about Social Services. Have you heard anything from them yet? Isn't there anything we are entitled to in our position? I know we're getting Child Benefit, but perhaps we could get more help.'

That was true. What with dealing with the children's adjustment to a new country, their emotional and health problems, and trying to chivvy everyone back in the Philippines, I hadn't thought about chasing up any handouts. But now, thinking about it, we had spent thousands of pounds on trying to get justice for Steven, and suddenly here we were caring for two young children.

The next morning I phoned Social Services, who said they

would send me a list of private nurseries. 'Private?' I queried. 'But I haven't got a job.'

'Sorry, Madam. You're not classified as a "family in need".'

'My son's been murdered. His wife has abandoned her children. We are struggling financially and psychologically. I need respite from Joshua, and I need legal advice about guardianship or adoption. How can you say we're not in need?'

The woman on the other end of the phone was embarrassed, but she explained that as I was not abusing the children, I was not a drug addict and the children were outwardly healthy and being well looked after, we simply did not qualify for resources that were already stretched. So we dug deeper into our savings and paid for a private nursery and legal advice.

A fortnight or so later we went to visit Jose, Juliana and their three-year-old daughter Lina. Now officially classified as asylum seekers, they had been given a house in North Yorkshire for which they paid neither rent nor utility bills. I could not believe my ears. On top of this they received £145 a week for food and other expenses, and another £48.40 to meet their daughter's 'dietary and cultural needs'. Lina had been given a place at a day nursery and had a hospital appointment for dental treatment. They had at their disposal a solicitor, barrister, social worker, interpreter and mentor – all within the space of a month.

I was furious. Not at this simple Filipino couple who were genuinely in danger in their own country, but at the injustice of the system in my own country. Here I was, a professional taxpayer all my working life, now being flatly refused services for Joshua. All we received on top of the basic Child Benefit was £9.15 per week 'Guardian's Allowance'. Jessica was on a waiting list for dentistry. I was a law-abiding resident of the UK and I was being discriminated against. How could this be?

My next tack was to try the Criminal Injuries Compensation Authority. This is a government-funded organisation that helps victims of crime, and I read up on them with interest. Apparently they handle about 80,000 cases a year and pay out about £200 million in compensation. *To qualify you must be able to show you have been physically or mentally injured as a result of violent crime, and you can claim on behalf of yourself or a child*, the literature read. *Even if you were not obviously the victim, you still qualify as a 'dependent or relative' of a victim of violence who has died.* This was it, I thought. The children definitely, and myself probably – surely we qualified for something. I filled in the form carefully, but there was a major stumbling block. Because Steven died *outside* the UK we did not come under the scheme. If he had killed Evelyn in the UK, her family would have been given travel costs, accommodation, support and compensation. As for me, I had nothing – not even advice. In vain did I plead with the Compensations Authority, in vain did I protest to my MP, in vain did I rail against the injustice of the system. Justice could only be sought if I paid for it.

I felt abandoned and helpless, and started withdrawing into myself. For all Alan's support and reassurance, I knew in my heart that I was letting Steven down. I couldn't give his children the care they needed, and I had not got him justice. I was rubbish as a grandmother, worse as a mother. What was the point of me now?

14
The Third Gunman

Looking back, I think I was probably clinically depressed. I just wanted to sleep, to blot out the world, retreat into a blank, dream-free place where there was no hurt, no responsibilities, no children requiring attention, no complicated legal system to navigate. Quite simply, I had had enough. I would struggle out of bed each morning and go through the motions of getting the children up and dressed, fed and to nursery. Once I got back to the house, I would slump in front of the television in a kind of trance. Sometimes I would cry, but more often than not I just sat and stared into the middle distance. I managed to rouse myself to collect the children, but it was Alan who coped with most of the shopping and cooking. When the children were in bed I forced myself to think about the case and what I should be doing to help.

It didn't help that things were not going well. I had lost my informant, of course, for Juliana was now in Yorkshire. Information had to be gleaned from Steve's friends and colleagues, from my lawyers and from the embassy in Manila. The police wanted to interview Martin's girlfriend Jennifer, but she apparently wasn't able to attend the hearing – I guessed she was afraid. As a Tagalog speaker she was crucial to the trial, so I put pressure on Martin to persuade her. The other key witness, Aurora – the maid who had given a statement testifying to the relationship between Evelyn and Adoray – had gone into hiding. My lawyers failed to find any other strong witnesses who could stand and give similar information. I was afraid of being arrested for kidnap, so that left only Martin. In February I was given an ultimatum by the judge: if I failed to appear the case would be adjourned, leaving a weak case against Adoray and Dagami, and Evelyn and Palabay scot-free. Clutching at straws, I asked my lawyers to see if they could do a deal with Dagami. Assuming he wasn't the one who fired the shot, perhaps he could be induced to testify that Evelyn was the mastermind behind the murder. I was prepared to offer a financial incentive to save myself from having to appear in person.

Time and again I asked the same questions I had been asking the previous August: 'Why has Evelyn not been questioned about the murder of her husband? Why did she not want to take action after his death? Why did she sleep with the killer? Why has her brother-in-law fled? Why did she argue with Rosario in Arnold's house? Why did she pawn her wedding ring? Why did she terminate her pregnancy after Steven's death?' Why couldn't the police ask her these simple questions? Alan might well keep telling me that Evelyn was innocent until proven guilty, but I was in no doubt that I had the answer. She was definitely behind his murder – nothing else made sense.

To: Margaret Davis
From: Christian Aguera
Date: 20 February 2003

Evelyn has been given three dates to appear in court but has failed to show up each time. The fiscal has ruled in your favour, that she is implicated on the evidence of the maid and her aunt, and the British Embassy is pressurising the City Prosecutor to include Evelyn and Palabay in the current case. Two hearings this month have been delayed because the lawyer for the two accused did not show up because of stomach-ache. We are looking into the possibility of Dagami becoming a state witness following your suggestion. There is another hearing on 10 March, we are running out of options for witnesses. If you cannot come they may 'rest' the case. Sincerely, Aguera.

If he could guarantee my safety from arrest I would go, but he could not. A few weeks later Aurora contacted me, which I was pleased about. We needed her to testify in person, and perhaps she could become my new informant.

To: Margaret Davis
From: Aurora
Date: 15 March 2003

Hello Mam, remember me? I need help and I hear you come to Angeles. I come out of hiding to find you but I afraid of Evelyn, she angry and come after me, so I need money to return to my family. God bless you. Aurora

To: Aurora
From: Margaret Davis
Date: 16 March 2003

Dear Aurora
Yes of course I remember you, and I am grateful for your help in making a statement about the murder of my son. We must see that the murderers are punished. I will come to the Philippines if there is a trial of Evelyn, but not before, and I will help you if you promise to continue helping me.
Margaret

To: Margaret Davis
From: Christian Aguera
Date: 20 March 2003

Dear Mrs Davis
We are glad to report that the court has finally received the

recommendation for the inclusion of Evelyn and Roberto Palabay in the pending case. The judge has not yet released the warrants for their arrest because he wants to be furnished with the picture of Palabay that was shown to Jennifer when she identified him. The police are searching for the picture in their files. There is one final date for you to present at court as witness, 26 March, and if you do not appear the court will use only the evidence they have. Sincerely, Aguera.

I so badly wanted to be there, but I wouldn't go until I was sure Evelyn was behind bars. The best way to achieve this was to continue to try, by all means available, to tag her to Arnold and to try to get Roberto Palabay to give himself up. But even I could see that we were running out of time.

Finally, I had some good news. The judge had signed an order to include Roberto in the trial, and there was a warrant for his arrest. He remained unconvinced that there was enough evidence to arrest Evelyn, although he was prepared to include her as a witness in the trial. My lawyers were charged to collect sufficient evidence and present to the court in the middle of May. Good news that they were after Roberto – although they'd have to find him first. And as for not having enough evidence to arrest Evelyn, I was speechless – she refuses to come in for questioning and still doesn't get picked up! I couldn't believe that this trial was proceeding in such random fits and starts, but the complicated workings of the Filipino legal system were way beyond my comprehension. In England the police collect evidence, the solicitor puts the case together, the trial date is set, the barrister defends or prosecutes, then there is a verdict. Simple. I had no frame of reference for what was or wasn't happening in Makati; I simply had to trust that a fair trial of all the suspects would happen eventually. Meanwhile I suggested to my lawyer that they use Steve's colleague

Miguel to help them locate Roberto. This was a good move, for a few days later I had a very interesting telephone call from Christian.

'Mrs Davis, I would like to report from my meeting with Miguel. We met him and Aurora's relative, Mario, who had helped in retrieving Joshua. He had also spoken at that time to Roberto about giving himself up in order to be a witness.'

'Yes, and as I recall Roberto kept changing his mind. Via Juliana I told Mario it was important to focus first on getting Joshua out,' I responded.

'OK, so this is our plan. According to their sources, Roberto is working as a fisherman in the village of Samar. Mario will conduct a surveillance of his day-to-day activities to determine where he lives.'

'Is Mario happy to do this?' I asked.

'He is nervous because his family believe he was paid millions to convince Evelyn's father to hand Steven's son to you. He does have some conditions, and I'll come to these in a moment,' he said.

'What do you intend to do after discovering where Roberto lives?'

'We feel that, instead of involving the local police, we should hire the NBI from Manila to serve the warrant of arrest. In our experience, the NBI are more professional and less susceptible to local politics.' I knew by this he meant bribery and corruption.

'Aren't they expensive, though?' The NBI were some kind of private police force.

'Yes, we think the whole cost will be 70,000 pesos but they will do the job. After Roberto is arrested Mario will try to convince him to become a state witness and confess the truth in exchange for his freedom.'

I liked this plan. It was the best way to get good enough evidence to present in court, and I was well aware that what they had so far – although clear as day to me – would not hold water without witnesses.

'Can you find other witnesses, in case the plan to entrap Roberto fails?'

'We can try, who do you suggest?'

'Carmen, Roberto's wife and Evelyn's sister. She knows a lot, and if you think about it her life is in a right mess now. Perhaps Mario can persuade Evelyn's father to get her to talk when he is in Samar. I know all of Evelyn's family are disgusted with her.'

'Right, we'll try that. Now I should tell you about Mario's conditions.'

'Go ahead,' I said.

'He wants Jose and Juliana to return to the Philippines before he conducts any surveillance.' I was stunned – this was pure spite.

'That is impossible. I am happy to pay him for his work, but he cannot ask for these people to return.'

'There is much jealousy amongst the people of Angeles that this couple has a safe haven in the UK.'

'They risked much to rescue my grandson, and this was a reward from me. I can't get involved in everyone else's jealousy. Mario cannot make these conditions, and I don't feel we can trust him if this is his attitude. I have never been in direct contact with him so I feel unsure about him. Perhaps you should contact Marcelino, the local elder, who acted as the district policeman in Daram Samar. He was reliable before when he told us about Joshua's whereabouts, and he may be able to get to Evelyn's father.'

Christian agreed to try this tack, and he also thought it would be wise to apply to the court for additional time to gather more evidence.

I felt a little better after this conversation – it seemed that at last something was happening. But the more I thought about it, the more convinced I was that Mario was not the right person to send. I did not like his attitude. It took my lawyers several days to contact Marcelino and when at last they did, he agreed to help find Roberto. They also had a copy of the warrant of arrest. More progress.

To: Margaret Davis
From: Christian Aguera
Date: 27 May 2003

Marcelino has located Roberto in Western Samar but has not yet made himself known to the family in case Roberto disappears. We will keep you informed.
Yours, C Aguera.

Now that the net was closing around Palabay, the fog in my head began to clear a little. I was far from being back to my old self, though, still lacking interest and energy and feeling like a zombie half the time. It was very hard to motivate myself to look after the children properly, but Alan stepped in and would take them for long walks in the nearby forest, returning with jars full of bugs and beetles. On top of everything Jessica was having dental problems. She had complained of pain soon after arriving in the UK, and when I looked in her mouth I saw to my horror that several teeth were blackened. How could this be? She was only four. Eventually the long-awaited dental appointment came through, and the news was grim indeed. It seemed that Evelyn used to give them sweets and fizzy drinks, and had not taught them to brush their teeth: Jess had to have six teeth pulled. The poor little thing was faint with pain, but never made a sound. What had this mother done to her children that they were afraid to complain? I hugged her so much that day, holding her tightly by my side – but perhaps more to give myself comfort than her. She still needed a great deal of reassurance, and I often found myself sitting in her nursery-school teacher's office discussing the best way to handle her. After two terms she remained reluctant to join in with large group activities, and remained as an observer, always watching the other children rather than playing with them. She gave various snippets of information about her past to the adults working there, as if she was seeking out people who could explain the meaning of her story to her, but she stopped talking about it with me. I wondered if she was trying to protect me, or if she thought I would be angry at her? There was so much work to be done with her emotions, and I knew we were only scratching the surface. And the more I read about grief, trauma and shock, the more I realised the journey ahead would be long and rocky. For both of us.

When I wasn't occupied with the million little things that make up a domestic day, my mind kept coming back to the same thought. I felt cut off from information about what was happening in the Philippines – not hard practical information, such as I received from my lawyers, but soft, gossipy information – the kind that we really needed to draw out key evidence that would reveal the mastermind behind the plot to murder my son. I needed a new informant, preferably a woman, who could move discreetly through the community without suspicion. I thought about Rosario's daughter, Aurora the maid, but she had gone into hiding. Who else might I try? I racked my brains. Then I remembered Maria, the wife of one of Arnold's security guards, who had been friends with Carmen, Roberto's wife. She might just know something. I set about trying to obtain her mobile phone number.

Through a complex network of colleagues at Steve's office, and bar girls of Maria's acquaintance, I eventually got hold of her, and over the next few months she became my informant, sending me text messages rather than emails. As she gradually opened up to me, I discovered that she had vital information. According to her, Evelyn had instructed Carmen not to tell the police that she had been with Arnold on the day that Steve was killed. She returned home at 4 am on the back of Arnold's bike, and told Carmen to say she had been at home all night. So my suspicions were confirmed. If only she would testify to this! But I knew all about family loyalty, and this was Evelyn's sister. She'd never squeal, I was sure. Maria, however, thought differently. She also convinced me that Mario was trustworthy, and could be used to get to Carmen to persuade her to testify. In recognition of this new information, I wired money to Maria for her, Rosario and Mario, and let my lawyers know what I was doing.

'Alan, I think we've had a breakthrough,' I whispered, just after I had completed the financial transaction. I hardly dared to speak out loud. 'Maria thinks we can get Evelyn's sister to testify against her.' I was excited, and I wanted everything to happen right now.

'That's brilliant, love, well done. But there's still a long way to go. Let's not get our hopes up yet.' Ever the voice of reason, my Alan. I couldn't sleep that night, not from anxiety but because my mind was whirring with plans and schemes.

Night after night, I sat at my desk in Bingham, texting Maria and Mario in Angeles, Marcelino in Samar village, and emailing my lawyer in Manila. Keeping them all interested, motivated, and with just enough money to get things done (too much, and they'd have no reason to carry on) was like juggling more balls in the air than I knew how to handle. I prayed that none of them would come crashing down, and kept in mind my guiding principle: that the only way to get this resolved was to work the Filipino way.

It was similar to the time when I was arranging for Joshua

to be rescued from the province. Difficulties arose daily: the long journey to Samar – two days by road, and half a day by boat; fears of violence from members of the families of the two accused men; fears that Roberto's family would have guns; constant requests for more money; offers to deal with it all swiftly by bumping off Evelyn. Another piece of news from Maria disturbed me: Evelyn had a new boyfriend, a policeman. She had used him to get a warrant to claim Steve's company car, which she then sold. Was this cop somehow pulling strings to keep her out of trouble? It might explain how she had so far evaded questioning. This case was getting murkier by the day, and more than ever I needed support from my people on the ground. I prayed I could trust them. I kept reminding everyone that they would be rewarded as soon as the case was complete. And I was determined to play fair: no way was I going to stoop to Evelyn's level. Years ago, when I was studying management, my tutor had said something that stayed in my mind: 'View a problem like a game of chess. Anticipate your opponent's move, allow it, then develop a plan to intercept the next move. Always stay one step ahead.' This was what I was doing now.

The lawyers got an extension of time to the end of June to present more evidence.

Text from Maria 14 June 2003:
Job has been done. Roberto is caught, in our control. It was very dangerous to get him, we found him in jungle, he was fighting to get free. We have the NBI with us now to arrest him and take him to Tacloban jail, but we have to hire a boat to get there.

I exulted in this, and called my lawyers to ask for confirmation. They explained that there had been a local fiesta in the province, and what with the music, dancing and general chaos it had been a golden opportunity to nab Roberto. We would have more news after they arrived in the next town. I would not have been so happy had I known what nearly happened. Luckily I heard after the event:

Text from Mario 15 June 2003:
We had very bad journey, boat nearly washed away by typhoon with us and NBI in it. All very frighten. Now OK in Tacloban, Roberto OK to testify.

That was a close shave; I knew those little banka boats, they were only eight feet wide and not more than twenty-five feet long, powered by a small outboard engine. Hardly robust enough to weather a rough day on the South China Sea, let alone a typhoon.

Following this, I established that Marcelino and Mario were working together, but they were concerned for their safety. The next target was Carmen, and I advised them to use the NBI if they needed to, and to expect some expenses from me. Every time I contacted them I emphasised that what they were doing was to get justice and to get a guilty person punished. I knew I had to keep them motivated – and reiterated constantly the importance of justice and truth. Would I manage to break the fiercely strong family code of honour with calls to their conscience? Or was it the promise of filthy lucre? Either way, I felt my goal was within reach.

The lawyers were feeling rather pleased with themselves, and sent me a large bill. It included costs for air travel for all the informants and the NBI – and even the suspected third gunman, Roberto. In the covering letter the lawyers boasted that they hoped soon to be able to arrest Evelyn, who they had heard was on a remote island called Palawan. I would believe this when I saw it, and I felt credit was rather more due to me than to them, but I paid their bill nevertheless. I still needed their help.

A few days later I had a text from Mario asking me to call him urgently. 'I am sure Roberto will testify,' he said, the line very poor, 'but I am very afraid now because family of Evelyn very angry with me for working for white woman. Family say Evelyn innocent and Steve's mum stole the children away.'

My heart sank. The family was closing ranks after all.

'So why are you so sure he will testify?'

'Because he say Steven good guy. He buy a boat and build a house for family in Daram and the family want everything of Steven's.'

'What about Carmen?'

'Mario and Marcelino, we go back to village to see Carmen. God willing, she will talk.'

'OK, I am pleased with your work, you are doing a good job for me and Steve. I will keep my promise to you and pay you for this good work. But Carmen must talk.'

'Ma'am, we may need guns. We really afraid.'

'No, Mario. You must do this without violence.' No way was I going to sanction firearms.

'People can be killed in this province, and no one will know. Comrades of Arnold and Dagami know we have Roberto, they send us threats.'

'I will talk to my lawyer, and he will help you. I do not want a death on my conscience.'

I didn't want to worry him, afraid as he already was, but I hoped he would be quick. My concern was that Evelyn would hear of Roberto's arrest and use her police boyfriend to help her disappear. There were many places to hide in that country. Christian assured me that he would send all the necessary support.

The next day I received some disheartening news. Having been interviewed by the NBI, Roberto was not after all prepared to turn state witness. Instead, he produced a statement written by his wife Carmen claiming that he had nothing to do with Steven's murder. Rather extraordinarily, she blamed Roberto's grandfather. Later, Roberto said his cousin did it. So they hadn't got their stories consistent; the only positive news.

That same day I heard from Marcelino that apparently Carman *was* ready to testify against Evelyn, but that her parents were refusing to allow her to leave the province, fearing for her safety. He and Mario were still prepared to try to persuade Roberto to turn witness. I was on tenterhooks, not knowing what to believe, not daring to hope for anything – these people changed their minds like the wind. For several days I waited without news, barely able to eat, firing off texts and receiving no answers. In the end I received a surprising request from Mario.

'Ma'am, Roberto wife is here in Marisol, she crying and desperate for your help. She needs money for a lawyer for her husband in jail.'

'Why does she need my help? Can't she ask Evelyn? She has some money.'

Evelyn did have money. I had heard from Maria that she had sold some land that rightfully belonged to Joshua. When he was born, Evelyn had asked Steven for £10,000 to buy some land in her home province as an investment for Joshua. Steven agreed, knowing that foreigners could not buy land, and although he would not have chosen this particular spot he felt that the impulse to buy her son some land was a good one, and he encouraged it.

'No, she afraid Evelyn will kill her,' came the reply from Mario.

Right. I tried to get this straight in my mind, which was spinning with anger. Had I heard this correctly? Was I really being asked to supply a lawyer to the man who quite possibly murdered my son? I had paid for the privilege of his arrest, and now I had to pay for a defence lawyer to fight my own prosecution lawyer? I was gobsmacked. Here was a woman who had helped her husband hide from the law, and who had kept quiet about what she knew about the murder. What kind of twisted country was this? I was pleased she was crying – it was her turn now. I didn't imagine she had given *my* tears any consideration. No, I would not help her. No way was I going to fund Palabay: he either gives up information voluntarily, or he is tried as a murderer. However, it was important not to let Mario know what I was thinking.

'I will talk to my lawyer, Mario. In the meantime try to persuade both of them to confess what they know. Where is Carmen now?'

'She is staying with Maria.'

I started to text Maria. Work on Carmen, I said, be gentle. She will turn, I feel it. Remind her that Steven's ghost will not rest until the guilty people are brought to justice.

It worked. At the end of June I had this text exchange with Maria:

> Maria: *Carmen wants to tell about the bad things Evelyn planned to do to Sir Steve. Mama Rosario told Carmen to tell the truth, she is elder sister. Evelyn father cannot sleep he says Steven's spirit is on his shoulders.*
> Margaret: *What will Carmen say?*
> Maria: *That Evelyn told her that she and Arnold checked with a lawyer, who said they would get a million pesos if Steven died.*

What a stupid, ignorant girl, to believe this – and then to act on it! What she hadn't done was think it through. If she had asked, 'And if I kill him, will I inherit?' or, 'If there is another beneficiary to the will, will I inherit?' the answer would have been very different. This must have been the legal aid lawyer who ran that radio station.

Margaret: *But Steven gave Carmen and her family money for food and medicine.*

Maria: *Evelyn promised Carmen more when Steven was dead. Ma'am, I need money to feed Carmen and her children. Carmen sad when Steven die because he was humble and good husband of Evelyn.*

Margaret: *You have done well, Maria.*

Maria: *This I believe is miracle, for sister to become witness against sister. Carmen she cry all the time, and Evelyn father he sick in his heart.*

Huh, so Carmen wanted forgiveness. Could I afford to be magnanimous? Her husband was in jail, and her family was feeling the pressure – a daughter implicated, a son-in-law in custody. I knew I had to keep calm or risk spoiling the plan. I decided to send a little money, bit by bit, for Carmen. Her children were, after all, Jessica and Joshua's cousins, and they lived in raw poverty. But by God, I was angry. It was all very well for her to want to talk now – she had held her tongue for Evelyn on the promise of a cash payout. So many people knew what she was planning, and Evelyn must have bought their silence.

Margaret: *OK, I will send money. But first Carmen must testify. Tell her that her heart will be free when she tells the truth and helps Steven to rest.*

I gave this information to the lawyers, and waited for the results of the next hearing. Meanwhile Roberto was not happy in jail. He was in the next-door cell to Evelyn's lover, and, according to my informants, was being threatened by him. He was refusing to talk for fear of reprisals – and quite understandably so, for inexplicably Arnold was present when the police came to interview Roberto. Arnold was apparently surrounded by a group of thugs, his 'bodyguards', who would do his dirty work for him. Already up for Murder One, what did he have to lose if he killed another man? The guards turned a blind eye to the shouted exchanges from one cell to another – they had nothing to gain from keeping an inmate alive, I guessed. But I had. I pulled all the strings I could to try to arrange for a transfer to another jail, but I was told he would have to request this at his arraignment, two weeks later. I feared for his life.

One day I decided it was time I spoke to Carmen – I knew I'd find her at Maria's house.

'Carmen, this is Margaret.'

'Oh.' A long pause. 'Hello, Ma'am.'

'Are you OK, Carmen?' I wanted to sound friendly. 'I have been thinking about you. I am sorry for you because your husband is in trouble. You and the children will always be family to Jessica and Joshua.' As a woman, I genuinely felt for her in this situation.

'Ma'am, can you forgive Roberto?' She sounded as if she was crying.

'His were the eyes that showed Arnold Steven's sleeping face. Steven was the innocent one. Roberto can help himself and his family by letting his conscience tell the truth.' I didn't say I would forgive him, I couldn't think about that yet.

'I am glad you have the kids,' she responded. 'It is good they are with you.' Why, oh why didn't she warn Steven? This woman, more than anyone, could have saved his life. I wondered if she would have been so contrite if the plan had worked and Evelyn had cashed in on Steven's wealth. I stifled my feelings and merely said, 'Carmen, it is important for you to give a statement with what you know. Evelyn has taken Jessie and Joshua's daddy, I don't want her to take your children's daddy too.'

'Yes, Ma'am. I want to tell the truth,' she said in a small voice.

Carmen gave a sworn statement to my lawyers later that month. Then it had to be presented to court, after which I assumed they would issue a warrant of arrest. But, as I had discovered, the simplest things sometimes take the longest time. Then came the report from Roberto's arraignment. After all our carefully laid plans, because of the death threats he was receiving he pleaded not guilty. Therefore, because he was denying any involvement in the case, he was deemed unsuitable as a state witness. Arguing their case, the lawyers claimed that as soon as he was transferred to another jail his plea would change. One step forward, another step back, I thought gloomily, and – it was becoming second nature now – emailed Peter at the embassy to ask him to help push this transfer through.

Finally, at the end of July, Roberto was duly transferred, and I crossed my fingers that all would now go to plan. What a daft idea, Margaret! For no sooner had this happened than I received news that Maria and Mario were all getting threatening text messages, warning them to stop Roberto and Carmen testifying. I was getting in very deep here, and felt frightened for them. Annoyed too, at the same time, because money I was sending was not being shared out as I had requested.

At the pre-trial hearing a few days later, Roberto finally agreed to talk. I still have the copy of his statement, and it makes chilling reading.

A week before Steven was killed, Evelyn talked to Arnold Adoray about having Steven killed since they were no longer getting along, so that Evelyn and Arnold could live together. I know Arnold Adoray since he is the branch manager of Silver Wings Security Agency where I used to work as a security guard and because he is Evelyn's lover. On the night of July 17, 2002, while my wife and I were resting in our room in Evelyn's house, Evelyn approached me and told me to come with her. I did not ask her where we were going. I just put on my clothes and prepared to leave. Outside the house I saw Arnold and Alexander Dagami who were waiting inside a white car. They asked me to ride with them in the car where Arnold handed me a .38 revolver. Alexander, also a security guard, also had a gun with him. At around 11pm the four of us left Angeles in the car and travelled to a place unknown to me. Arnold and Evleyn sat in the front, and Alexander and myself in the back. After a few hours we stopped in a street. Arnold and Alexander got out and told me to go with them. Evelyn stayed in the car. We walked towards a house. Arnold opened the gate of the house using a key, and opened the door of the house using another key. Once we entered the house Arnold and Alexander drew their guns which made me very nervous because I couldn't understand what was going to happen. I followed them while they went up a flight of stairs. First Arnold, then Alexander, then me. When we reached the top of the stairs Arnold told me to stay by the door near the stairs while Alexander opened a flashlight. They both entered a room. It was dark and I was confused and I switched on the lights near the staircase. Alexander left the room and went towards another room where he also called for Arnold. Both of them entered the second room and after a few seconds I heard some gunshots. I looked into the second room where I heard the gunshots and saw Steven full of blood with his hands raised while Arnold was still pointing his gun at him. Right after, they left the room. We hurried down the stairs. We went back to the car and hurriedly left the place. While we were driving back to Angeles City, Arnold and Evelyn told me to keep quiet and not to tell anyone what I had just witnessed.

What shocked me most was not the matter-of-fact tone of this statement, in which cold-blooded murder was described as one might recount a meal out. Nor was it the dramatic insight it gave me into my son's last moments – I had, after all, imagined this scene hundreds of times. When I had seen the photographs of Steven I had realised there were moments when he must have raised his hands, pleading for mercy – and as I had suspected, Martin had give me the 'kind' version. No, what shocked me was the admission that Evelyn was there. Somehow I had always imagined her elsewhere. Yet she was there; she sat calmly outside while her husband was murdered in his bed at her own request.

She was there.

This crucial news meant that I had been right all along. Despite my instinct from the very beginning that she was behind this, I had always had a small doubt, a small nugget of hope, that it wasn't her after all. I ached for my poor, betrayed son. And the knowledge of her evil-doing gave me renewed strength to fight on.

15
Burdens

It was August again. A whole year since Steven had gone from my life — a year in which I had changed from a contented grandmother with the next twenty years sorted to a bitter, driven mother-of-two with a vengeful mission. So much had happened in the past twelve months, yet sometimes it seemed only moments ago that I had received the dreadful news.

The children had broken up for their summer holidays, and we started to see an improvement in them. I think they were happy in the warmer weather, it suited their dispositions and they were naturally inclined to strip off and run around the house and garden in nothing but their pants. Jessica made friends with the little girl next door, a confident child named Olivia who was loud and boisterous — the polar opposite to my timid Jessica. Still, I thought, it might bring her out of herself a little, and I encouraged them to play together in our garden most days. My proudest moment that year was during one of Jessica's dental appointments when she informed the dentist that I was her new mummy. She still constantly looked for reassurance from me, craving affection and love, as if silently begging me not to blame her for her mother's sin.

As for Joshua, he was much easier to handle now, and had made some friends at his nursery. He was at last beginning to smile without frowning, but I still found it hard to shake off my negative feelings towards him. Things he did would remind me of when Steven was a baby — little mannerisms, the way he held his spoon and fork, the way he neatly arranged all his toy cars in lines. 'Such a handsome little boy,' people would gush, but sometimes I could hardly look at him. At other times I would hug him so hard he couldn't wriggle away – the feelings of love, hate and guilt continually fought each other in my mind. We hadn't had a party for his second birthday in June – I simply hadn't been able to celebrate anything back then – so to make up for that my daughter Lucy and my sister Gillian organised a tea party for him now. With Lucy dressed up as a clown, and traditional party games like musical bumps and pass the parcel, it was a riot. I noticed how the local kids threw themselves into the activities with gusto, while our two small exiles seemed dazed and confused. It was as if they had both been reborn in another country, and everything was new to them. Even a birthday party.

Like them, I was also staying on the sidelines. Still on tenterhooks for news of the trial of Adoray and Dagami, still to hear whether Evelyn had been questioned, still providing a drip-feed of money to my informants and still receiving text messages from them. The strain of this left me emotionally wiped out and financially drained. One afternoon I was sitting in my usual place – at the computer – looking at the statements from Western Union, the bank I used to send money overseas. I was trying to do a rough calculation of the money I had spent over the year. It was already over thirty thousand pounds. Catherine was over at our house visiting the kids that day, and I turned round to see her at the door, hands on hips.

'Mum,' she said bossily, 'don't you think you should slow down now?'

'Slow down? What do you mean?'

'Well, you've got the kids, you've got Roberto Palabay in custody, can't you let the authorities over there just do their job?'

'It's not that easy, Catherine,' I said, surprised. 'Haven't you paid any attention to what's been happening over the past year? The so-called authorities will do nothing if I am not on their case'.

'Who do you think you are, Erin Brockovich? You can't single-handedly run this investigation.'

I willed myself to stay calm. 'If I let go now that will be the end of it. I would hope you could be more supportive, you know how important this is to me.'

'That's as may be, Mum. All I know is that I feel I don't know you any more. I miss the old Mum.' She paused, then blurted out: 'And we haven't even had a funeral for our Steve.' Suddenly she left, muttering about making tea. She knew she'd overstepped the mark, and clearly wanted to escape. I sat quietly and thought about what she'd said.

She was right: we had not said a proper goodbye to Steven. Alan and I had been at the cremation, but my girls and the rest of the family were also grieving and hadn't had the sad but necessary ritual of a funeral to mark the end of grieving and the beginning of acceptance. It was my problem, I knew that perfectly well. But I wasn't ready to part with Steven's ashes, and perhaps that meant I wasn't ready to accept the fact that he was dead. His ashes were in my bedroom cabinet, where I could see them every day. Sometimes I spoke to him, told him what was going on with his case. And I had promised myself that he would rest when we had complete justice. Now I realised that my quest for justice was hurting my children, and perhaps hurting Alan too. Had they all been discussing me behind my back? Catherine clearly thought I was obsessed. Was I? I thought I was just determined. I was an emotional wreck, it was true, and I found it hard to think of much else. I would wake at night and feel as if I was going out of my mind. Maybe there was a kernel of truth in what she was saying.

I turned off the computer and went down to the kitchen, where I found Catherine busying herself with the teapot.

'How's Jack?' I asked, hoping to have a normal conversation with her about my grandson, whom I seldom saw these days. In fact, I realised with a pang, no wonder she's sore.

'Don't change the subject, Mum.'

'What do you want from me?' I asked in desperation.

'Nothing – just for you to go back to how you used to be.' Ah yes, if only. How wonderful that would be. Alan and I used to take Jack and Lucy's son Joseph every weekend, and often during the holidays. I called them 'my boys' and we had some magical times with them. I smiled as I remembered how I used to email Steve photos of our latest exploits. 'Hope my kids will get as much of you,' he once said – and I wasn't unaware of the irony of this long-ago comment. Indeed, it was to redress the balance a little that we had planned to sell up in the UK and build a large house on one of the Filipino islands just south of the mainland.

'You're so wrapped up in the trial and missing Steve and doing everything for his kids. Your mind is elsewhere, you're never here, with us. What about the rest of your family?' Catherine was saying, but I sipped my tea and thought about how things should have been.

'We'd have been there by now, you know,' I mused. 'Last time we went Steve had the owner of the island mow a strip of land so he could land his plane there.'

'We wouldn't have seen much of you if you'd moved to the Philippines. But now you're here and even in death Steven is still taking you away from us.'

'Look, Catherine, I'm your mother and I love you all. How many pieces can I split myself into? Can't you put aside your sibling rivalry and help me get through this? I'm sorry for the state I'm in, but I can't help it. I desperately want things to go back to normal, and maybe they will eventually. But I can't do it alone.'

'OK, Mum. I'm sorry.' She came over and hugged me. We were both silent for a moment, then she said brightly, 'How about us girls all go out to bingo one night this week? We'll let the men look after the kids and we'll go and blast those balls.' I laughed. 'Good idea, it would be great do something normal for a change.' And it was – my spirits lifted enormously, and I think that girls' night out was the first time I had actually enjoyed myself since Steven died.

That month I had some good news.

To: Margaret Davis
From: Christian Aguera
Date: August 7 2003

We write to inform you that the court has decided that the evidence of the prosecution is sufficient to shift the burden of proof on to the accused.
Sincerely, Aguera.

This was a tipping point in the case – it meant that the evidence the court had seen so far, all the statements from my witnesses, was so stacked against the two accused men that it was now up to Adoray and Dagami to prove that they *didn't* kill Steven, rather than our having to prove that they *did*.

I called Martin to update him on this, and to let him know that I had also heard from Maria that Evelyn was living in Bataan province.

'Suits her. It's a vile and dirty place,' he commented. 'Where exactly is she living, do you know?'

'Maria says she's living at Ronnie's house.'

'Ronnie?' he asked.

'The gay guy who used to come to Steve's house and walk

around in a bra and nicks. Apparently he was the one who introduced Evelyn to Arnold.'

'What about Palabay?'

'He gave a statement, and said it was her who showed them the house, gave them the key. She was there when Steve died. And the police have statements from her sister, aunt and cousin. They can't fail to pull her in now, surely.'

'When they do we can have a proper celebration. Hopefully over her rotting corpse.'

'You're still angry.'

'Yeah, the past year has been pretty bad. Living with the memory of witnessing and hearing your buddy shot dead, and wishing you could have done something about it. I'll never shake it off. I just want to see Steve avenged and you satisfied. And I'd like to know why they left me alive.'

'If they had shot you, Evelyn would be living happily ever after with my support and Steve's money.'

'I live through that night every day of my life; it's changed me for ever.'

'Martin, I have wondered about this time and again. Was there any point at which you could have shouted out to Steve, could have woken him and warned him?' I couldn't help it, I had always had this nagging suspicion that Martin could have saved his friend.

'I've asked myself the same thing. No. I think I was just in shock, I was numb. And I was terrified.' I couldn't imagine what it would feel like to have a gun at your head. Perhaps Martin feared that if he shouted out they'd come and finish him off. The instinct for self-preservation is the strongest instinct of all.

'I understand.' I didn't really. Martin was alive and my son was dead.

'Don't give up the fight for justice, will you?' he said.

'No, I'm a stubborn so-and-so who doesn't like anything

stolen from her, especially her children. I cannot begin to put this behind me until they are all caught and punished. Evelyn will have to live the rest of her life with the knowledge of that night, just like us. I have to wake up every day to the knowledge that my son is dead. She wakes up without her children.'

'Good luck Margaret, keep me posted.'

Poor Martin, he was suffering the same pain as me, but in his own way. I thanked God he had been left alive to be our witness.

Later that month probate was finally granted on Steven's estate, and I was able to put his money into trust for his children. The estate was handled by the solicitor I had asked for help very early on – the one I had known since his days as a councillor. Throughout the months of correspondence on the estate he never once asked me how I was coping, or how the children were getting on. I felt he knew he had let me down and was studiously avoiding the issue. He was not the only professional person to avoid crossing emotional boundaries; it seemed that it was easier for them not to risk saying anything. What were they afraid of? That I would break down in front of them? A thoughtful word or letter from time to time would have cost so little and would have meant so much to me. I could not shake off the bitter feeling that I had been abandoned by officialdom.

I was getting no joy from my previous MP Ken Clarke, so I tried Graham Allen, the MP for North Notts. He was sympathetic, but said he could do very little, other than prove to me what I already knew – that I wasn't entitled to any help from Social Services. He had also been informed by the DSS that I had brought Joshua into the country illegally, and that he was regarded as an 'asylum child'. This was news to me, and quite incorrect. The confusion amongst British authorities rivalled the incompetence of their equivalents in the Philippines! I was still hoping to find out if I was eligible for something called kinship fostering, but Social Services remained silent on this point.

Then one day I read a report in the paper about the family of a girl who had been murdered in China. The grieving family had struggled to find out what had happened, but had received no help from the authorities either in China or in the UK. It all sounded horribly familiar. At the bottom of the article a support group was mentioned: SAMM. The acronym stood for Survival after Manslaughter and Murder. At last – here was an organisation whose sole purpose was to help people like us. Alan and I went to their next meeting which was specifically aimed at those whose relatives had died abroad. We were overwhelmed by what we discovered. In an atmosphere charged with grief, frustration and anger, parents, brothers and sisters crowded into the hall to hear each other's stories and to exchange advice. One key theme emerged above all others: we all felt abandoned. We had all discovered that the Foreign Office had no policy for people like us: there was no legal assistance, no compensation, no support. We – the law-abiding, taxpaying families of the ninety-five souls murdered outside the UK each year – were the disenfranchised.

The feeling that you are not alone in your troubles is a very powerful one, and this was the first time since Steven died that I felt I had any support. Spurred on by this, I decided to take my complaint higher and wrote to the Foreign Office, and to the Minister, Baroness Symons. I now knew that I was not the only person to be dealing with the murder of a relative outside the UK. The way we had been treated pointed to very many failures in our system, and I not only wanted to ask for help – particularly as I knew I would have to return to the Philippines eventually for the trial and I did not want to be arrested for kidnap – but also to prevent anyone else from suffering the same treatment. These, in essence, were the points I made to her:

1. I was never informed officially that Steven had died – I heard about it from his business partner and the newspapers
2. I did not receive advice on how to bring the body home or have an inquest
3. I have never received any kind of support – practical, legal, emotional, financial – in the UK, and have never had any contact with UK police
4. I was not eligible for benefit because I had savings and no drug or alcohol problems. I was not even eligible for a foster-care package
5. Victim support was not available to me because my son was murdered in a non-European state
6. As a Westerner I was seen as affluent and was therefore vulnerable to people hoping to profit financially from my misery and need for justice
7. The Filipino police seem reluctant to pursue the case against Steven's wife, despite four testimonies from people implicating her. How could I, a grieving mother in Bingham, push progress? Would I have to pay the judge himself next?

I begged her – and the Foreign Minister Jack Straw – to consider the fact that foreign nationals who arrive in Britain needing help are rightly given whatever support we can offer, whereas as a family of British nationals, I had found there was no safety net for us. I had nowhere to turn. I urged her to look at putting together a package of support for people in my situation. Was it too much to ask for people like me to be informed, supported, given practical help? I felt this was reasonable and long overdue – particularly in view of the new social mobility that meant that many more British people were now working and living all over the world. I also wrote to the Home Office Minister, Lord Bassam, who was conducting a review of the fairness of the Criminal Compensation Bill, but I never received a reply.

I also applied for a judicial review of my case with the Criminal Injuries Compensation Scheme, based on the assertion in their manifesto that *Payment of compensation is intended to be an expression of public sympathy and support for innocent victims*. What was I, if not a victim? Was my grief and pain so different from others' whose relatives had died? Surely we should not be dismissed because of where Steven died. Surely there should be a system that identifies human rights equally and without prejudice. My appeal failed, and with it my belief in the great British sense of fair play.

Finally, I wrote to the President of the Philippines, Gloria Arroyo, who was considering reintroducing the death penalty to reduce overcrowding in prisons. The way I saw it back then was very simple: a life for a life. My views have since changed, but I did not understand then why Steven's murderers should be living while Steven was dead, and I encouraged her to have the strength of her convictions and bring back the death penalty. I was not surprised to receive no reply.

This is how my life was that year. I would experience huge bursts of energy, driven by a fierce anger and a sense of injustice, and then these would be counterbalanced by long periods of inactivity and depression. The halting progress of the investigation – one step forwards, two steps backwards – didn't help. I found it very hard to keep a handle on what was happening in the run-up to the trial of Adoray and Dagami – the whole process seemed convoluted and confused. Witnesses wouldn't turn up, hearings would be delayed, the defence lawyer had another trial, the judge had passed a motion seeking more information, someone else was ill . . . there was always some reason for things not happening. Depending on the news I had received that day I would either be fired with hope that the end was in sight, or downcast and desperate, sure that justice would never be achieved. I loved the children passionately, but I resented them too. I was inordinately grateful towards Alan and the rest of my family for stepping in to help, but I was angry at myself for not being able to cope, and for the sarcastic little comments I would let slip. My exhaustion and ill temper would come up against what I saw as Alan's silent condemnation of my obsession with the case, and arguments would erupt after the children were in bed. Above all, I wanted what I could never have again. I wanted to go back to how things used to be. And I wanted my son.

My letters did eventually bear some fruit. I was contacted, albeit fourteen months later, by a police liaison officer, who accompanied us to London for a meeting with the Foreign Office. This officer had obviously had a great deal of experience with bereaved relatives following violent crimes, but at this stage it was a case of too little, too late. We had been invited to meet David Brierley, someone high up at the Foreign Office, and found him most cultured and kind. He gave us an unequivocal apology, and promised to keep us informed of events during the trial. He accepted that we had not received adequate information or advice when Steven died, particularly as we could have been in great danger ourselves when we travelled there at the outset. Following our meeting he wrote: *I regret that we failed to follow our preferred procedures, and we fully accept that our service to Mrs Davis at the time of Steven's death was lacking.*

It's funny, but the mere fact that we received this apology made me suddenly so much happier. Looking back on what we went through during those early weeks, now knowing that I was right to feel aggrieved and abandoned – not merely paranoid and stroppy – meant a great deal to me.

Early the next year I received a reply from Baroness Symons. She acknowledged my position and understood my complaints, and talked about raising the question of wider support for those affected by murder overseas. I felt she valued my comments and would genuinely review the services provided by the consular offices. One day, I promised myself, one day – when all this was over – I would think seriously about taking up the cudgels on behalf of victims such as myself. But for now I had done all I could, and I was using all my reserves of energy on fighting my own battles and bearing my own burdens.

While these letters were flying around we were waiting to see what the two accused men would come up with as proof that they did not kill Steven. Sure enough, they both claimed to have alibis. Arnold's alibi was a woman who had supposedly heard him coughing at midnight on the night Steven was killed and had given him cough syrup in the early morning. The court pointed out several inconsistencies in her story and, frankly, did not believe her. Dagami's alibi was his claim that he was working as a night guard for another security company at the time and could prove it with the log of his working times. The judge decided that the log was a fake and that as the company was not registered it did not exist. I gave a hollow laugh – to think that they'd imagined cough medicine and a few entries in a notebook would get them off Murder One. These two were a few sandwiches short of a picnic.

'Alan,' I announced after hearing this news from my lawyer in Makati, 'I think we can allow ourselves a small celebration.' He looked at the email.

'You're right, we're well on our way now to a proper trial for these two. With Palabay's statement in and Carmen's not far off, surely it's only a matter of time.'

Suddenly full of hope and excitement, we arranged for Gill and Lucy to have the children and checked into a hotel for a couple of nights. It was blissful, and a chance to talk and plan. For some time I had been feeling that the children would benefit from being brought up in a warmer climate, and my disaffection with the UK system was turning me against my own country. I was also fed up with Jessica's nursery: they had organised a multicultural day the previous week and had dressed her up as an Afro-Caribbean girl. I was furious – of course it's important to teach the kids about different cultures, but at least let her acknowledge and celebrate her own background. It was during this weekend that I had a bit of a brainwave.

'Let's move to Spain with the children,' I said to Alan.

'Blimey, there's no stopping you, is there Marg?' he laughed, not taking me seriously.

'I mean it, Alan. Think about it – we know the country a little already from our holidays, the kids are always happy there, it's a relaxed way of life. And Spain did rule the Philippines for hundreds of years – there's a cultural connection too.'

'Steady on, love. We can't just run away from England. What about my job? We've spent so much on getting justice for Steve, I can't chuck my job in.'

I nodded and said no more, thinking that I'd leave the idea to germinate and perhaps Alan would come round.

Shortly after this weekend away, Carmen gave her statement. A shiver ran down my spine as I read it. Carmen had two small children of the same ages as Joshua and Jessica – she was often in the house with Aurora helping Evelyn out and I had got to know her quite well.

I am the older sister of Evelyn Davis, the wife of the deceased Steven Davis, who was killed last 18 July 2002.

I first met Steven Davis in 1998 when he was introduced to me by my sister, Evelyn. During the time that Evelyn was pregnant in 1999 I stayed and assisted her at their home until she gave birth. I went back and forth between their house and my relatives' house. Last 2002 I learned that Evelyn had a boyfriend in Angeles City named Arnold Adoray. I went to see Evelyn and asked her if what I heard was true. She denied it at first. However, last June I heard from our relatives that she was having frequent fights with her husband, Steven. When I heard this, I visited her to see how she was doing. During our long talk she told me that she and Steven were always fighting and that she was not given money for household expenses, even though his business was doing well. She also admitted to me that she had a relationship with Arnold Adoray. As her sister, I advised her to sort out her problems with her husband. In the course of our conversation, Evelyn talked about her anger towards Steven. She even revealed to me that she and Arnold Adoray had plans to kill Steven. When I asked why, her answer was so that they would be free to live together and appropriate the wealth that Steven Davis would leave Evelyn. I scolded Evelyn and counselled her not to pursue with her plan but she said nothing. In the belief that Evelyn was not serious with her plan and that she said the same only out of her anger towards her husband, I just left after we talked. In August 2002 Arnold Adoray dropped by our house. I was surprised when he informed us that Steven was shot and killed inside his house in Makati City. We later on went to the wake in Angeles City in order to mourn with Evelyn. While at the wake, I remembered the things Evelyn told me, but because of fear, I just kept silent. I execute this statement for the reason that I am being bothered by my conscience and in order to help unravel the truth behind Steven Davis' killing.

I was sickened at the betrayal I read of here. Carmen had known what Evelyn was planning. Mama Rosario had known too, as had Evelyn's parents. How could no one have warned him? Why did no one stop her? Carmen had kept quiet on the promise of receiving money from Evelyn, and none was forthcoming. Only because I was sending her money for her children did she now agree to tell the truth. I felt my anger rising but I knew it was a waste of energy. At least this brought us a step further on – a motive for the murder, and another witness to the relationship between Evelyn and Arnold.

Although we had these two new statements, neither witness had appeared in court yet, and my informants were still receiving threats. I would get daily pleas from them to have Evelyn arrested. I was sure it could not be far off, and I reassured them that we were nearly there. How wrong I was. I found myself fantasising about Evelyn and her accomplices hanging from a noose for her crime.

To: Christian Aguera
From: Margaret Davis
Date: September 3 2003

Can you tell me what the likely sentence for murder is if they are found guilty?

To: Margaret Davis
From: Christian Aguera
Date: September 4 2003

Madam, in our country it is 40 years for murder. The death penalty is for heinous crimes like kidnapping, rape and drug-related crimes. This could be an exception because of the nature and pre-meditation of the murder. We hope because of good

I shook my head in disbelief upon reading this. Yet another
example, I felt, of the topsy-turvy nature of justice over there.
How could murder be seen as a less serious crime than
kidnap or rape? That had to be wrong, surely.

I heard later in September that Evelyn was planning to
escape to the island of Palawan with her boyfriend. This was
bad news. She would be very hard to find – that was where
the missionaries we had read about the previous year had
gone missing. Only their heads were found, several months
later. Not a nice place.

I kept up the pressure on my lawyers for news on the
mystery warrant for Evelyn's arrest, but was told that there
was evidence that she had been in Angeles at the time of the
murder in Makati. I wondered where this could have come
from. What we needed was for Palabay to be officially made
a state witness, and this could only happen once a motion
had been passed. God, it was frustrating. The wheels of
justice were turning so slowly they were almost going backwards.

To give them their credit, my lawyers were now sending
me regular reports concerning the various court hearings that
were going on towards the end of that year. These hearings
were spread over several months, and were subject to many
delays. I received one report from a hearing at which Dagami
was questioned. He claimed that he had confessed to the
crime, but only under police torture. On being asked why he
had not mentioned this before, he replied that he had
forgotten. Forgotten that he was tortured! I laughed at this;
surely no one would believe him. Yet again his claims to have
been working for another company were ripped to pieces,
particularly as one of the dates he gave as having been

assigned to guard Evelyn and Steven's house was the day of the wake. His so-called defence did him more harm than good.

That Evelyn had another boyfriend by now I knew, but nevertheless I was shocked to hear from Maria that she was expecting a baby. A baby! My heart went out to this half-sister or brother of my Jessie and Josh. Another innocent caught up in Evelyn's twisted adult world – what would become of the child when she was thrown in jail?

One night, unable to sleep, I sat downstairs on the sofa leafing through my cherished photograph albums of Steven, and particularly those covering the years he spent with Evelyn. The gorgeous young couple at their wedding in Hong Kong; Steven and Evelyn embracing on beaches and on top of mountains; Evelyn cradling their first child; Jessica's first birthday; Joshua's arrival . . . so many photographs, all lovely happy shots. None gave away the canker at the heart of the family; none revealed the ugly heart of this beautiful Filipina girl. As I turned the pages, my tears fell. How could she have destroyed this wonderful life? I reached for a pen and started writing a poem.

Steven Davis 1970–2002

His first crime was to love you, sincerely with his heart.
His second crime was to cherish you, and hope you never part.
You killed him with a heart of stone born of your lust and greed
And he died alone, of this you gave no heed.
But the worst of crimes that you have done is abandoned your daughter and your son.
My life, your life, our future hopes and dreams, are stolen to the past:
The love desired for another was never yours to have.

But now the time has come to pay for what you have done.
For the crime you did by God and law is a punishable one.
With your life and soul God may in time forgive, but your
    children never can.
For they will know the truth of why their father died so
    young.
So go to hell forever –
In a prison you will abide
With your lover and the guilty ones burning by your side.

The next morning I looked up Evelyn's address in Bataan,
given to me by Maria, and sent this poem to her with pictures
of all of us – her 'family tree'.

I wanted to remind her of what she had thrown away.

16

The Gunmen Come to Trial

This is how things stood as we came towards our second Christmas without Steven: Evelyn's lover Arnold Adoray and his co-conspirator Alex Dagami came to trial in November 2003, fourteen months after being first imprisoned. The trial would take three months. They had been held on the basis of Martin's testimony and identification, and the evidence of Evelyn's cousin and maid Aurora and her aunt Rosario – both of whom had testified to the relationship between Adoray and Evelyn.

The third gunman, Roberto Palabay, had been on the run for eleven months since Steven's murder, and had finally been arrested in June 2003. It had taken me months of persuasion via intermediaries, and a constant flow of money, to ensure that the key witnesses appeared in court, to get him to a position where the authorities could negotiate with him. His evidence was to be instrumental in getting the two convicted, and he would not have given this evidence if I had not asked his wife Carmen to persuade him to grass the others up.

Thanks to my unremitting pressure on the authorities in the UK (and no doubt I was becoming a bit of a thorn in their side) I had been promised that a member of staff from the British Consulate in Manila would attend each court hearing and report back to London. No longer did I have to pay for information, no longer did I have to put my trust in possibly unreliable sources, no longer did I have to operate in a cloak-and-dagger fashion. Proper communication had now been granted to me, and I felt rather as that Greek bloke who used to lift the world up on his shoulders must have done when he gave it to someone else to hold for a while. But I still had one unfulfilled objective. Evelyn. I was convinced that she had killed my son. Why was she still free?

Nonetheless we were determined to have a good Christmas with the children and put the last seventeen months behind us. We invited Jose, Juliana and their daughter Lina to spend a few days with us: they were too afraid of repercussions to return home, although as Catholics Christmas was an important family time for them. Jessica and Joshua were showered with presents, my sisters and daughters did all the cooking, and I did not have to do anything. I spent most of the week alone in my room, missing my son more than ever. For unhappy people, traditionally joyful times such as Christmas are all the more poignant.

As December turned into January, my contacts in Manila, Angeles, Makati and the provinces were becoming more and more anxious, and as the trial was starting I received daily, panicky text messages from Maria, Mario and Roberto:

> *The family of Adoray and Dagami are making trouble for us.*
> *If Adoray goes to prison they will want to have revenge on us.*
> *Evelyn's boyfriend is member of NPA, they very bad people and I am on their hit list.*
> *Madam you must not come here the NPA is angry with you.*

The New People's Army was a well-known and deeply feared group. This news rattled me considerably – was this why the police had been reluctant to question Evelyn, I wondered. The prosecution had filed a motion for her arrest several months before, but the judge had decided that there was insufficient evidence to arrest her. Mentally I urged the trial on. I heard things were not going well for the two men, and I felt that the sooner these two were convicted, the sooner the evidence would point to the brains behind the crime. If not, we would have to wait until Roberto Palabay was questioned. The trial dragged interminably – there were innumerable delays and postponements, which, the Foreign Office was at pains to point out, were not unusual by Philippine standards.

It was in February 2004 that the defence lawyer finished, and it was the turn of my prosecution team. Remember that this was a civil action brought by me, the complainant, and led by my private lawyers. Their first witness was Carmen Palabay, Evelyn's sister. She gave her damning evidence. The following day her husband, Roberto, turned state witness.

No sooner had he given his statement than the judge pronounced the two men guilty. He sentenced them each to thirty years and ordered them to pay 50,000 pesos each to Steven's heirs. At the same time he issued a warrant for Evelyn's arrest. Steven had been dead almost nineteen months.

At last.

To: Margaret Davis
From: Christian Aguera
Date: 17 February 2004

We write to provide you with an update on Evelyn's arrest. She was arrested in the village of Zambales, a 12 hour journey by car from Makati, and has now been brought to the Makati City Jail where she will be detained while she is being tried. Three officers from the Warrant Section of the Makati City Police accompanied one of our associates. Her two month old baby is being cared for by the relatives of her boyfriend in Zambales. We shall enquire from the Court when her trial shall be scheduled and shall attend to find out what her plea is.

I tried to picture the scene of Evelyn's arrest, imagining her in a run-down village with a baby on her hip. In my mind's eye I could see her pretty face contorted with shock and fear. I wondered if she struggled, or tried to hide, or whether she accepted her fate. I wondered if she spared poor Steven a thought. But most of all I thought about this baby. Was she still breastfeeding it? It was Jessica and Joshua's half-sister or brother – what kind of a life would it grow up to have? I was afraid I knew the answer. Would my two grandchildren ever meet their half-sibling? How would they deal with the gulf in their own experiences and opportunities? I can't pretend I wasn't delighted that Evelyn had finally been arrested, and there was great rejoicing in my house the night we heard the news – particularly as Evelyn's first night in jail coincided with the birth of my new grandchild Hollie, Catherine's daughter. Martin telephoned in a state of great excitement – he had heard the news and had gone into the police station to ask the officers what had happened. Apparently she had betrayed no emotion when she was arrested. 'She was very cool,' they had said. I believed it. This woman had no emotions.

As for me, more than anything I felt a crushing sense of pity for this other poor baby half a world away, already deprived of one parent.

To: Margaret Davis
From: David Brierley
Date: 17 February 2004

I am very pleased that there has finally been some significant progress in the murder trial. However I must ask you to consider carefully any decisions to travel to the Philippines in the foreseeable future. Our Consul in Manila and I feel it is our duty to warn you that it would be unwise to travel as your safety cannot be guaranteed. Should you enter the country, you are liable to arrest for the abduction of Steven's two children, no matter your good intent for doing so, which we fully understand. It is possible that Evelyn herself intends to turn your removal of the two children against you, and press charges of abduction in the courts. Additionally, as you are aware, there may be various parties in the Philippines who may turn violent against you and Alan. Reports of revenge should be taken and treated with caution.

Kind Regards, DB

Evelyn's hearing happened a few days later, and I was advised that the trial would commence in sixty days. Nothing would stop me from going out for the conclusion. I had unfinished business with Evelyn and I was determined to see her one more time. Naturally the judgement day was delayed several times, but I was ready to drop everything and go as soon as I was given a date. The spring and summer passed slowly.

Meanwhile I continued to keep in text contact with Maria. Carmen and her children were living with them, and although her husband had been released as a result of his having turned state witness, he was in hiding for fear of reprisals. I continued to send money through my lawyers to several people for food and expenses, and to make sure they stayed involved in the hearings at Evelyn's trial.

These months were very significant. It was a time of hiatus, of waiting, but also a time of reflection. I had first been approached about making a documentary the previous March when Arnold and Dagami's trial had been reported in the UK media. I hadn't been able to decide whether to go along with the idea or not, but the producer Katinka Blackford Newman had kept in touch, and I spent a long time considering whether to go ahead with this: after all, it would represent a real intrusion into our private grief, and my initial reaction was to say no. At length, after Adoray and Dagami had been convicted, I decided that it would be the right thing to do. Alan and my daughters were immensely supportive of this decision. We would not receive any payment, but we would be documenting the truth for the sake of the children.

But by God it was hard. Katinka was unfailingly professional and I liked her enormously, but the experience of putting the documentary together was an intensely emotional experience. She asked me to do a visual diary of Steven, by which she meant I should piece together significant moments in his life with photos, mementos, videos – in short, anything that would make an impact onscreen. I was fortunate in that I had so much material on film, partly because of Steven's love of technology and habit of cataloguing every experience. Watching them all again brought back so many happy memories, sad as it was to watch them. But I needed to go back further, to his childhood.

And so it was that I found myself in the attic going through the piles of little things I had saved over the years. Photos, paintings, short stories, school reports, and in amongst them three small shoeboxes, labelled 'Catherine', 'Lucy' and 'Steven'. I had almost forgotten about them but I knew what would be in them: all those precious little things that only mothers keep.

I sat for ages, hugging the box, hardly daring to open it, feeling my heart beating with anticipation and longing. Eventually I lifted the lid, and the first thing I pulled out was a card: *Congratulations on the birth of your baby boy, love Mum. 27 March 1970*. I stroked the card lovingly, tears streaming down my face. I remembered his birth vividly: I had lost two babies before him, and was hospitalised late in my pregnancy to make sure everything would be all right. My precious boy: so hard to get; so easy to lose.

Another card, from him this time. It stopped me from looking at any more that afternoon: *Happy Mother's Day, Mummy. Lots of love from your favourite boy Steven.* Felt flowers had been carefully stuck with lots of glue on the front, and he had covered it with masses of xxxxs. His wonky writing was that of an enthusiastic eight-year-old. I closed the box, not knowing if I could continue with this process – the memories were too wonderful, yet too painful. I knew I was not the only mother ever to have lost a child. How on earth did other people cope? Was it like this for them all?

Over the next few weeks I found more and more memories. And out came the photos – the girls in the Brownies; Steven; their dad Joe, my mum and their cousin Dean aged about three. Of these six people, four were already dead. How vulnerable I felt. It was the face of little Dean that captured my thoughts – as a child he had spent so much time with our family that I had treated him almost as my fourth child. He was my youngest sister Sharon's boy, and as she was only sixteen when she had him, it suited all of us for him to be included in our family as much as in hers. Dean looked up to Steve as an older brother, always admired him. The poor lad had suffered with depression as a teenager, and had been troublesome to his mum – but with us he was easier, and Steven I think helped him greatly. Eight months after Steven died, Sharon found Dean hanging on the stairs. He was twenty-five years old. At the time I had regarded his death as yet another casualty of Steven's murder, but while I was working on the documentary Sharon said something interesting, but poignant. She told me that Dean had said it would be safe to die because Steve would be waiting for him.

* * *

I was keeping busy with all the demands the researchers and assistant producers were putting on me, and in a way it felt comforting to be documenting Steven's life. Of course at times it was unbearably painful, but other times it was helpful in many ways to draw various things together and give some meaning and shape to his life. It calmed me to be able to recall all the little events I had forgotten, and it enabled me to feel that he was still very much with me. It didn't make his death any less random or pointless, but I think I started to see his life as a whole, rather than as a portion of what might have been. And I drew the conclusion that all these precious memories meant that I was a lucky mother indeed to have shared so much with him, and if the memories bore tears then so be it. At least I have a rich stock of them that I should be grateful for.

Katinka and her team went to Manila to interview Evelyn. She denied everything hotly, of course. The documentary shows a little of her life in custody: lying on her bed doing nothing, wearing the unattractive yellow uniform, singing some sort of official song with all the other inmates. They then went all the way to Daram Samar on one of those rickety little boats to film her family. I was on tenterhooks all the while Katinka was gone, fearing for her life. There were plenty of people, after all, who did not want that film made, and it would have been the work of a moment to tip the film crew into the sea. I was relieved to receive her call when she returned to Manila, but worried about what she said.

'Margaret, I couldn't believe the utter, grinding poverty of the place. I want to do something to help those children. What a shocking environment for Evelyn to grow up in. No wonder she wanted to escape.' Katinka was very upset, deeply moved at the desperation and the sickness. This was all true of course, but hang on – what about the task in hand, I thought. Are you losing your focus? I feared that the documentary would take an overly sympathetic view of Evelyn. I should not have been concerned: it did in fact present a very fair and balanced view of the people and events. Many people told me how moved they were by it.

Katinka knew that Evelyn's trial was approaching, and managed to attend some of the early hearings. She was well aware of the great television opportunity my presence at the verdict would be, but she also knew of my fears about attending. Every time we spoke she asked me what my plans were. Secretly I always knew I'd go – how could I miss it? But my problem was persuading Alan, and when he decides to put his foot down he does it emphatically.

'You're not going, Marg. No way. It's too dangerous. You know what the penalty for kidnap is. I'm simply not allow-ing it.'

I nodded, hoping that by the time the question arose again he might have softened a little. But no, he was implacable. Then I was able to give him some news from my lawyer.

'Alan, Christian Aguera said he's checked with every judge in the country whether there are any warrants for my arrest. And he says there are none.'

'How can he be sure? It's still too much of a risk. What would I do, with you in jail? Would you put me through that? And what about the children – haven't they lost enough already?'

'I really want to go, Alan. I don't think they'll have me up on a kidnap charge. Even if they do, I'll talk myself out of it.'

'You've got Palabay. He's nailed her, she'll definitely go down for this. You don't need to go.'

Yes I did. I knew I had to see Evelyn one more time, and I wasn't going to pass up this chance.

To: Margaret Davis
From: Christian Aguera
Date: 10 October 2004

The verdict on Evelyn Davis will take place in Manila courtroom on 25 November. Sincerely yours, Aguera.

To: Christian Aguera
From: Margaret Davis
Date: 10 October 2004

I will be there.

17
Judgement Day

'When we going to Auntie Gillian house?' asked Joshua, now a bouncy two-year-old.

'Tomorrow, Josh, pack your toys up,' replied Jessica happily. 'We're going to stay for three whole days. It's fun at Auntie Gillian's house, she lets us have chips and ice cream and videos and things.' She bustled around him, collecting up his Bob the Builder set, ever the organising big sister. I smiled. I knew my sister Gill spoilt them rotten, but I also knew I could trust her: they were completely safe with her. It was late November 2004, and Alan and I were preparing to go back to the Philippines for the first time since that first horrendous trip just after Steven died. After more than two years, we were returning to see the murderer brought to justice. Or so we hoped. I was tense and anxious as we packed, trying not to betray my feelings to the children. Luckily they were still young enough not to question why we were going away, or where we were going. I slept fitfully that night, waking every hour, checking the time on the digital clock as Alan slept. At last the light began to shine in through a crack in the curtain. 5 am. The journey to Heathrow and the long flight lay ahead. There was so much to do: I hauled myself out of bed and made a cup of tea. My head was all over the place; I needed to focus. I took refuge in writing a list of things to do.

As we said our goodbyes to the children later that day I broke down. I couldn't bear leaving them – a simple thing like saying goodbye just pushed me over the edge. They did not know I was going to see their mother, and how cruel it would have been to tell them, but something in me wanted to take a little bit of them to her, and to bring a little bit of her back to them. How I wanted them to have their mummy back, these precious little children who hardly remembered the exotic creature who had cared for them when they were tiny. If only I could erase her terrible crime and bring her back to love them again, if only I could make their shattered world whole again.

'Come on, love, the taxi's here.' A tight-lipped Alan ushered me into the waiting car, and I managed to wave at the children through my tears. They carried on waving back at me until the car rounded the corner. I closed my eyes and thought of my dear Steven. Here I was again, going to the land he so loved, knowing I would not find him there. I wondered for the millionth time what the verdict would be. Would Evelyn be set free? Would they believe that she had been coerced into it by her boyfriend? Or that she knew nothing about what was being planned? Surely not, yet I had been warned that it was possible, and I knew for certain she would demand the children back and have me up for kidnapping. How ironic that would be – we go to her country to see her jailed, and end up with death sentences ourselves. I knew we were taking a huge risk by returning to the Philippines. I knew we were defying the authorities, from the police to the Foreign Office. But I had to go. The circle had to be completed, whatever the outcome.

We arrived at the airport to find the television crew waiting for us. I had known they would be there, but still it felt like an intrusion. Of course they wanted shots of us 'starting our journey for justice', or something. In truth I had started my journey for justice the moment I heard my son had been murdered. Katinka, the producer, was brief with her questions, but they still took me by surprise and I groped for answers. At times I was unable to speak, feeling vacant and shut down. It was strange being the centre of attention with microphones and cameras pointed at me. How I wished I did not have to do this. Once on the plane I swallowed some Valium and tried to blot out the seventeen-hour journey we had ahead of us, the journey we had done so many times with excitement and pleasure.

'What's your contingency plan then?' Alan asked Katinka. 'What happens if Margaret is arrested?' He was still unhappy and nervous about my decision to go.

'I'll be there with the cameras,' was her response. I smiled to myself: being arrested was the least of my problems.

We eventually arrived in Manila and followed the mass of people through immigration, the baggage hall and arrivals. I allowed myself to go with the crowd, hardly feeling present at all. I was numb and tired, and suddenly at the exit the tropical heat grabbed my body and my mind went fuzzy. The sounds and smells were familiar, but confusing nonetheless. I fanned myself with my passport, feeling as if my body was being squeezed by the heat, unable to breathe. Alan and the crew were in front so I moved towards them, my legs like jelly. It was dark; it must have been around 8 pm, but I had no concept of time. We stood waiting for taxis, pushed and shoved by crowds of people moving in all directions. I looked into their faces, searching the Filipino features for one I had seen before, recognising all, yet knowing none. There were a few Western faces. If only one of them could be Steven's, if only. In my dazed state I almost saw his face through my blurred vision. Rocking back and forth on my heels, I smiled at the pleasurable thought that he was here to meet us. My Steven, he was here at last. Khaki shirt and chinos, hugging and welcoming me with great delight. I imagined his strong arms around me.

'Get in, Margaret.' It was Alan, guiding me towards the

taxi where the crew were waiting. I could have socked him one in the jaw for wrenching me from my delicious reverie. I would have given my life to have that moment with Steven again. My eyes stinging with tears, my heart bursting with too much hurt, I told myself to take deep breaths. I knew it would take all my strength not to break down. This was what I had worked towards for over two and a half years. I couldn't collapse now. I had to be at the trial the next morning. I had to be in the same room as Evelyn when the judgement was given.

Although we fell into bed crushed with exhaustion, we slept badly, through jet lag or anxiety or both. So tightly coiled were we with anticipation, we hardly remembered to be relieved that we hadn't after all been arrested.

'Well, today's the big day,' announced Alan the next morning, forcing a grin. 'Better get some food down you, you'll need to keep your strength up.'

'I know. It's going to be a difficult day, but I'm glad we're here.' Stay calm, I told myself, stay focussed. Keep your dignity.

We met the crew and headed for the court. I felt safe and protected with all these professional film people – they had been there already to do a recce, they had gained access and acquired permission for their presence in court. Unbeknown to us, there had been a great deal of behind-the-scenes work, and no doubt many palms greased to smooth our way. On that morning they needed to set up their cameras, lights, sound systems and so on, and we were very early. Alan and I decided to go for a walk around the building. It was opposite Manila police station, the one we had visited so many times. Memories of the time we had spent in that place came flooding back.

'Isn't this the same place that you gave your affidavit?' asked Alan.

'Blimey, you're right. Do you remember that strange silent man in that dark little room? I can hardly believe that was over two years ago.'

'Yes. It seems like yesterday.'

We walked on a little, and came to the town hall. 'Look,' I said, 'That's the same queue of people waiting for something or other. That's where we waited to get Steve's death certificate.'

'It doesn't seem possible. Where has the time gone?' Alan wondered, almost to himself.

It's strange how time stretches and contracts, telescopes and magnifies. In a way I agreed with Alan how quickly the time had gone, yet I knew that every painful step of this whole damn process had been excruciatingly slow, that I never thought the time would pass. I had sometimes believed that nothing would happen, that we would never get a result. And yet everything had eventually come to pass. We had managed to rescue Joshua. Roberto Palabay had been found and questioned, and had confessed. Adoray and Dagami had come to trial and had been jailed for thirty years each. The children had grown older, stronger, more confident. And now it was Evelyn's turn for trial. As for me, I had spent months in a dark and lonely place but I was coming through it.

'No, Alan, it has been a long, hard struggle. This place takes us back in time to the summer Steven died, but I'll never forget that every single day has been a mountain to climb. I remember him every day and miss him all the time.'

'God, I know, I didn't mean . . .' he faltered. 'Look. I want you to know, Marg, that whatever happens today, I am incredibly proud of you. I've watched you go to hell and back since Steve died, yet despite that you have kept a level head, you have been absolutely bloody determined to get justice for our boy, you have left no stone unturned. Christ knows how hard it's been – you've had setbacks and problems and all sorts of trouble, but you've done it. I take my hat off to you.' At this he doffed an imaginary cap and bowed low. 'And Steve would be proud of his mum, too. He's a very lucky chap.' I tried to laugh, but I was crying too much.

It was getting near to the time. We went back to the court building and found a small room at the side of the building. It looked like a run-down waiting room at a bus station. Was this where we were supposed to be? We stood around, the only white people in a sea of Filipino faces. It must have been obvious who we were.

Katinka came up to me. 'What if she is found innocent?' she asked.

'Then I would have to do what Steven would want me to do. If she is innocent he would want me to set aside what has happened and reunite the children with their mother. If she is innocent those kids will be back with their mum, with my full support.'

'Do you think there is any possibility that she is innocent?'

'No. None whatsoever.'

A short while later a large white van with bars over the windows pulled up. I shrank back into the crowd behind me so as not to be seen by whoever got out of that van.

It was her. I gasped and held Alan's hand tightly.

Head bowed, eyes cast down, not showing her face, Evelyn entered the room escorted by two mean-looking guards. Her wrists were secured behind her with handcuffs. As she came in I slipped out quickly, not wanting her to see me yet.

'Was that my mother-in-law?' I heard her say in Tagalog. So she had seen me, after all. Alan and I made our way up the concrete stairs to a balcony around the courtyard, and then into the court. It was a shabby room, poorly furnished, no larger than sixty square feet. There was a small table at one end for the judge, and the public were seated on wobbly benches on either side of the room, with a kind of aisle down the middle. Alan and I sat on the right side. Steven, are you here? Are you with me? This is for you, I thought. I felt his presence by my side, a warm breath.

Evelyn shuffled into the courtroom, wearing her dark glasses. 'Typical,' I whispered to Alan. 'She's always hiding behind those glasses.' The guard motioned her to sit at the front of the room on the left. We were just behind her, on the other side. There were no more than four feet separating us. She sat, head bowed; I guessed she was too afraid to look around at her audience. I couldn't take my eyes off her, drinking in every detail of how she looked. I had been expecting her to look her glamorous former self, rather as she had looked at the funeral parlour – she had always loved feminine, figure-hugging clothes and gold jewellery. But now she wore an old tee-shirt, dirty jeans and a pair of black trainers with orange stripes. Her hair was dull and tied back carelessly. I was shocked to see her like this.

We were close enough to see her breathing. She was panting, clearly frightened, and I thought I could see her heart pulsating in her chest. She seemed to shrink into the small square of wooden bench on which she sat. Was she thinking now of Steven, and the fear he felt as he realised he was going to die? Did she have any sympathy at all for the husband whose death warrant she signed? I turned round, thinking I would see familiar faces: her parents, her sisters, aunts and the many friends who were often at her house when Steven was at the office. There was none. In spite of myself I felt a pang of sympathy towards this girl, still sitting head down, all alone. She looked isolated, friendless, fragile. I wanted to reach over to her, hug her, hold her hand and tell her everything would be all right. She had been Steven's adored love; shouldn't I be loving towards her? Is that what Steven would want? No, she had betrayed him. My compassion fought with my knowledge of what she had done. This is the mother of my grandchildren, I told myself, and the love of Steven's life. Yet she is evil, she threw away his children and his life for the love of another.

Suddenly the court rose and I was wrenched back to reality. This was it. The judge entered. Evelyn's lawyer, a young man, spoke up for the defence. Then my lawyer summed up for the prosecution. I didn't understand more than a few words of Tagalog, but I could have written their scripts myself. There was a moment's silence while the judge considered his verdict. I kept my eyes locked on Evelyn. Then he addressed the court with the decision.

'Reclusion perpetual.'

What? I turned to Alan in confusion at the legal jargon. What did this mean? Was it the death sentence? I looked at the crew, who seemed equally bemused. I didn't want the death sentence for her. I felt betrayed by my lawyer and the judge.

Evelyn had fallen to the ground in shock. I thought I should go to her, but she was helped up by a guard, and after signing some papers, was led away.

'It means a life sentence,' my lawyer was saying as she left the courtroom. 'She will go to prison for forty years, no parole, no remission.'

I stared to my lawyer. 'Forty years?'

'That's right. I told the judge you were not in favour of the death sentence, and he was pleased that you were compassionate, not vindictive. You did not wish bad things for Evelyn.'

If only he knew. I was against the death penalty for Evelyn not because it was inhuman to take a life, but because I thought it was too good for her. I wanted her to suffer every day of her life for what she had done. I wanted her to wake up every day knowing that she would never see her children.

This is what it is like for me, and it is the worst feeling a mother can ever experience. She took Steven and now I have her children. Of course I wished her bad things: any mother would.

As we left the courtroom I noticed that there were guards in the waiting room. With them was Evelyn. I had to see her, I had to talk to her one more time, and no guards were going to stop me. I had loved this girl, I had cherished and nurtured her, I had respected her. She gave me two beautiful grandchildren but she took away my son. And she destroyed everything that was good in this world. For them as a family and for us as a family, she took my future and she took the children's future. I had to address these feelings with her.

So, with the protection and authority of the film crew, I marched in, suddenly calm and confident, suddenly possessed of a fierce determination to confront my son's killer.

She was sitting on the bench with her head in her hands.

'Evelyn,' I said levelly. She looked up, still wearing those blasted sunglasses. The same pair she had worn in the funeral parlour that day as she protested innocence. She turned her head away from me.

'Will you stand up, Evelyn?' I asked. She ignored me.

'Stand up and face me,' I demanded. I took her by the arm to help her up, and took off her infuriating glasses.

'Look at me, Evelyn. What have you got to say to me?'

'I am innocent, Ma'am. You know me, I loved Steven, I am innocent, innocent!' Her voice got louder. 'I am innocent!' She was almost screaming the word. I wanted to cry, I wanted to believe her, I wanted to put my arms around her, but I held back. My heart was thumping in my chest and my mouth was dry with anger.

'You put me here,' she screamed. 'You want someone to blame, you want my kids. It's all your fault I am here. I love my husband.'

At that instant any flicker of sympathy I still had for her, any vestige of affection remaining from my attempt to see her through Steven's eyes died. She was blaming *me* for the situation she was in! She had no respect or consideration for my grief and loss, no thoughts for her children's sadness, only selfish thoughts for herself and what was being done to her. No sense of her own wrong-doing, no feelings of responsibility or guilt, or remorse. I realised then that she was guilty and evil and cared only for herself. She had betrayed Steven and the children, she had no heart. For a few moments I was lost for words. I think I had expected her to beg for forgiveness and understanding, to cry for mercy, to ask about her children – and indeed, if she had done that I would have faced a real dilemma. Yet as it was she set me free from any fellow-feeling towards her. No longer did I feel responsible towards her. If I had ever had any doubt about encouraging the investigation or taking care of the children, I no longer had any.

'Evelyn, your family testified against you.'

'They lied.'

'Palabay confessed.'

'They are all liars!' Her voice was raised again.

I sat down next to her and drew a folder out of my bag.

'I have something to show you.' It was an album I had carefully put together for her, containing photographs of the children, photographs of her family and mine – in short, everyone she should have held dear. People who were now lost to her. She looked at it sideways, trying not to show me she could see it. I turned the pages slowly.

'This was Jessie's fourth birthday . . . here they are at Christmas. She cries for you, Evelyn. They have done some drawings for you, look. This is by Jessica and it shows you with the two of them. You are all crying, see those big tears? She needs her mummy, Evelyn. What am I to tell her?' No reply. 'Here is your father. My daughters. Your sisters. They despise you for what you have done. And here is Steven. Your husband. Do you think of him?' It was a picture of him in his coffin. Evelyn's face showed no emotion. 'What has become of your other child?'

'That has nothing to do with you,' she replied angrily.

'Oh but it does, Evelyn. That child is half-brother to Jessica and Joshua, and like it or not he does have a great deal to do with us.'

She yelled denials and accusations at me then, half in Tagalog, half in English.

'Was it worth it, Evelyn?' I was still speaking calmly above her shrieking. 'You have thrown away your whole family, your children and your new baby. And all for the love of someone who was not yours to have. Steven treated you like a princess. He loved you with all his heart. Your father once told me he was a proud man that you married a good husband. Now he is ashamed.'

She quietened down. It was time to go. As I left, I said, 'I will tell your children they had a beautiful mummy who did something very bad. She took their daddy's life and she had to pay the price. Goodbye, Evelyn, I will not see you again.' I left the album with her. Let her look on the pictures of her beautiful orphaned children and weep.

I left her sitting alone. She was left with what she had when Steven found her: nothing.

I suddenly saw through my tears as I left the room with Alan that there had been an audience throughout this exchange. People touched my arm in sympathy, smiling their condolences. This buoyed me up and I left with my head held high. I had said my piece.

Later that afternoon, drinking vodka in the hotel and crying with relief and exhaustion, Alan and I talked quietly about the day's events. It had been an incredible thing for any

parents to go through – to see their daughter-in-law convicted of the murder of their son, and then to be able to
confront her afterwards. We were both so glad it was all
over. Satisfied that she would now be paying for her crime,
but sad – so very sad – for the loss of the beautiful lives they
all could have lived, and for depriving the children of their
young parents. And it was all for nothing – Evelyn is not
with her lover. The children are not with their parents. She
chose to change her life and we have all paid a heavy price.
One image hung in my mind: our last goodbye to Steven, the
March before he died. She watched us hugging and smiling
and talking about the next time we would meet.

'This has been nothing short of a crusade for you,
Margaret,' said Alan. 'The cards were stacked against you
from the beginning, yet look what you've achieved. Your
instincts about Evelyn were right all along. Here's to you.'
He raised his glass.

'I couldn't have done it without you, my love.'

I felt as if a huge weight was lifted from my shoulders that
day. After two and a half years my final objective was
complete. The list I had only half ticked off when we brought
Jessica home with us was now all crossed out. Evelyn was
inside for forty years; Arnold Adoray and his accomplice
Alex Dagami had sixty years between them; Roberto Palabay
had exchanged his confession for freedom. I had to live with
this, although I did not think it entirely just: he was, after all,
the one who pointed the finger at Steven. The one who said,
'This is him.' Still, one hundred jail years in exchange for
Steven's thirty-two, the best Filipino justice could offer. Not
a fair exchange, but I hoped that Steven would look down
and smile, knowing his life had been avenged. I was certain
that if it hadn't been for my efforts, nothing would have
happened. The wheel had come full circle: this was the end of
a very long journey to justice, I had done my duty as a

mother, and now – finally – I could bury my son. Our future could now begin again. Not the future I had envisaged – my career was gone, we would have no retirement now – but I was determined to face it with optimism and energy. We had two very special grandchildren and we would do our utmost to help them grow up into strong, happy and loving people.

Epilogue

After Evelyn's trial I locked all my notes, diaries, letters and emails away in a drawer. With them I put photos, videos, pawn receipts, air tickets, hotel bills, computer disks – everything connected with Steven's death, the investigation and the trials. I wanted to put it all behind me, to move on with my life, and start living for the future instead of in the past. Somehow I could not destroy them, but I told myself that one day, when I was stronger, I would look at them again. That day came sooner than I had anticipated, when a publisher asked me to write my story. I remember sitting in the publisher's smart London offices wondering if people would really want to hear about the horrible things that had happened to us. Would I be able to do it? I was just an ordinary woman. Yet I really felt Steven was with me that day, urging me on. 'You can do it, Mum, I know you can.' So it was with some trepidation and a heavy heart that I took the great bundle of papers out, printed out emails, and sorted and sifted them into order. Indeed, it was thanks to Steve that I still had so much stored in the memory of my hard disk. And with all the documents my grief resurfaced. Reliving each step of what I call my 'journey to justice' was difficult at first, and I have cried a river as I had to picture my son's poor dead face again, remembering the children's tears for their vanished parents, the daily struggles we went through to help them become accustomed to new, unexpected lives. During the writing of the book the documentary was broadcast, and I was invited to do interviews for papers and the radio about my story. As it all flooded back to me and I mentally went through those years day by painful day, the grief that I had held back for so long for the sake of the children started to flow out. At long last I was able to be sad without feeling anger, and it felt good to cry, not wrong or foolish. So it was that with my tears my heart gradually began to heal.

I am still shocked at what happened; still appalled that the people who helped us get justice were the ones who knew of the evil lurking in Evelyn's heart. I never got to the bottom of why it took the police nineteen months to question her. I was glad to send them maintenance money while they were helping me yet justice, and I felt I was doing a little to lift them from the raw poverty of their lives. I still send money to Carmen and Roberto for their children, Jessica and Joshua's cousins, so in a way I am supporting one of the murderers. Carmen knows where their half-brother lives and perhaps one day they will meet him. Perhaps even one day they will want to meet their mother. She will be in her sixties when she comes out of prison, and they will be middle-aged.

We are living in Spain now. I think Steven would approve. It is a country with cultural links with the Philippines, for the Spanish invaded the South-East Asian archipelago some four hundred years ago and have had a long-lasting impact on the language, religion and culture. The climate is warm and, I think, strikes a chord of memory with the children, who spent their early months and years in tropical heat. With their colouring they even look a little Spanish. It is a wonderful environment for children, with lots of outside play, beaches, good schools, and a very family-oriented lifestyle where grandparents are accepted into children's lives rather more than they are back in England. I was overjoyed last Christmas to see Jessica and Joshua singing Feliz Navidad with gusto in their nativity plays. Indeed, it was the first normal Christmas we had spent since Steven died. They were excited about putting up the tree, something I had not done since Steven's death, and had fun making little things to put on it. We went shopping for presents for everyone they could think of, and surprised me with their knowledge of Papa Noel. Both of them are fluent in Spanish; Jessica dances flamenco at the local festival and Joshua is a chip off his dad's block – always busy and sociable and already computer-literate at his young age. We are very proud of Steven's beautiful and talented children.

Today they seem happy, but I am under no illusions about what lies under the surface. Jessica is eight now, but she still has bad dreams and what may be flashbacks. When I hear her scream in the night I am by her side in seconds, soothing her. I get the feeling that she is afraid of losing us too. Her favourite piece of jewellery is a delicate gold bracelet adorned with hearts and stars. She does not know its history.

'Why doesn't our mummy want us if she borned us?' I will never forget Jessica asking me one day soon after we moved to Spain.

'Do you mean our mummy from the olden days?' asked Joshua.

'Your mummy and daddy loved you very much. You were born in a hot country a long way from here. You have the pictures on your walls. But your mummy changed the rules, and she can't be with you now.'

'Why do you love us so much?' Jessica asked.

I went to the kitchen cupboard and took out the torch we always kept handy for emergencies. 'Look at this,' I said, closing the shutters. I shone the light through their closed hands so they could see the pinky-red outline of the blood.

'This is your blood. It is the same as mine.' And I shone the torch through my hand. 'We are family. I borned your daddy, and you are my grandchildren, just the same as Jack and Hollie and Joseph. You look different because part of you comes from people in that hot country far, far away.'

Questions like this come up every so often, and I try to deal with them honestly, and without any negative stuff about their mother. I know the questions will become harder as they get older.

Recently we were looking at a photograph of Evelyn and I said to Jessie, 'Isn't she beautiful, just like you.' 'Yes,' came her reply. 'Beautiful, but cruel.' Joshua, at five, is more straightforward in many ways – after all, he was not much more than a baby when he last saw his mother – but even with him we have tricky questions to answer. He often asks why I have a sad face. I notice how Jessica is drawn to young women the age her mother is now, and I know she craves the kind of mothering I am simply not able to give. I have in mind a couple of women of the right age to guide and help her when she hits her teenage years, and I have no doubt that for both Jessica and Joshua this will be a challenging time. I am pleased to see their strong bond with each other, and they talk often about their Daddy Steven who lives in the stars and looks down on them with pride. I hope that Alan and I are able to offer them something of the wisdom we have gained with our greater age, but we cannot be the young parents they should have had. We know we don't always have the energy we had when my kids were little. All we can do is our best, for as long as it takes.

They have not seen the documentary, and they will be much older when I allow them to read this book, but both, I think, will be vital anchors for them. Having been a social worker, I know children can grow into confused and depressed adolescents if they do not have a sense of who they are and where they have come from. The film shows video clips of Steven and Evelyn, and shows how they grew up in different worlds and met in paradise. We see them laughing and very much in love, we see them cuddling and playing with their children. Steven's humour and intelligence come across, and the film shows his friends talking about what a wonderful person he was, and their grief at his loss. It also shows their maternal grandparents and other members of Jessica and Joshua's Filipino family. Above all, it shows how the children were loved and wanted until their mother decided to take a lover. Her lust and greed for Adoray killed Steven; there is no other explanation.

So, if I am not around to tell them the story, the film and this book will help them know their history, their parents, and to learn the truth about what happened to them. I hope they will understand my reasons for agreeing to make the documentary, and for writing this book – it is my legacy to them. I hope, too, that this story will not only help my grandchildren, but that it will also offer some encouragement to other parents who lose children in violent circumstances, people who find themselves up against a wall of bureaucracy, or anyone who is facing the problems that can arise when the first world collides with the third.

I have a meaning to my life now. I have my children, I have Jessica and Joshua and all my other grandchildren and family members. And of course I have Alan, who has never doubted me and has been by my side every step of the way. Many men would have walked away from what I have put him through. I am usually happy. But being happy is not without its guilt: Evelyn was such a beautiful girl, and I am sad and angry she is not parenting her children. I did care so much about her, and even to this day I find it very hard to hate her. I haven't got the energy to hate her – how can I, when I love her children and they come from her? Missing Steven will never get easy, but I have come to accept the huge gap his death has left in my world. I talk to him in my mind, and I write poems about how I feel. I am a mother with a broken soul that simply can never be mended. I have learnt that grief has no pre-ordained path, as some experts will have it. The painful mixture of feelings is still there, and at times I still feel shock or denial, anger or hurt. Sometimes I feel I have accepted Steven's death; at others I still cannot believe it. Sometimes I feel a sense of peace and hope for the future, but sometimes I'll look at something Jessie or Joshua are doing and I think, Steve, just come back for five minutes to see your children. This will keep happening, I know. Steven's death is not something I will 'get over'; I am only starting to learn to live with it, and I accept these private moments of grief as and when they come. Anyone who has lost a child will know what I mean. It cuts so deep. A part of my soul has just gone out, disappeared.

I think the end of my story is that I have to gather my friends and family together and hold a proper memorial service to say goodbye to him. It is going to be hard to let go, as I have held his ashes close to me in their little white box for so long, but it is time. I know it is time.

On Steven's birthday each year, the children decorate helium balloons and tie little notes to the string, telling their daddy about what they are doing and how they are getting on. We go out to a windy hill and let them fly up into the sky.

'We love you, Daddy,' they shout. 'We miss you. We hope you are happy, wherever you are.'

Farewell my son. Not goodbye.

A journey for justice, a journey of faith
Is now left behind me
Love for your children is meant to last
But mine will forever be entwined with the past
A journey of justice now done with price
A journey where you always stayed at my side
But now it is time to put you to sleep
Knowing my son that memories are a treasure to keep.

I miss you so badly and now we are one
I now have a soul when I thought it was gone
So into the future with your children we move on
Some day together my beloved son
My heart feeling heavy, my tears burn away
As the sun lowered slowly over Manila bay
I know it is time to let you free to peaceful sleep
Knowing my son the memories are a treasure to keep
So farewell my son, not goodbye.

Mum
xxxxxxxxxxxxxxx